"EmotionalGRIT is a true calling for helping the next generation live beyond stories and circumstances, thus creating a shift in the world once we reframe our thinking."
GINA OTTO
ChangeMyWorldNow.org, CEO, Founder
International Best-Selling Author

"Emotional GRIT ignites a visionary future that craves a new generation of compassionate leaders to set the stage for a heart-centered evolution in humanity."
RAVÉ MEHTA
Grammy award-winning pianist
Producer and Bestselling Author

"Emotional GRIT is what men and women need, to understand the importance of being human, and regaining what it means to pause in today's fast-paced life."
ANTHONY TRUCKS
Former NFL Player
International Speaker
Founder of Renew University

"EmotionalGRIT should be a household name for anyone desiring to build their tenacity, character and strength-as a leader, partner, parent, and overall human being. Men typically aren't taught to understand their emotions; this book provides you the basis for how you can change that to enhance every area of your life. "
ERIK FULKERSON
CFO Elite Excursions

"EmotionalGRIT is pivotal to understanding the role of our emotional strength and is mandatory for the state of our mental health as well as for our optimal capacity as humans."
MATT RIEMANN
Founder, ph360.me,
The Human Foundation Projec

GW00497814

"This is the future of collaboration, when we move past our limitations and discover the potential to truly solve challenges in the world, which starts with mastering your Emotional GRIT."
DR. HARBEEN ARORA
Women Economic Forum, India

"Leaders & entrepreneurs have difficulty showing vulnerability which attacks the core of trust, Global GRIT is an opportunity to enable a different approach of thinking."
SANJAY SINGHAL
Founder of Audiobooks & Venture Capitalist

"Emotional Leadership as pointed out in Emotional GRIT is the future of preventative mental health and a bold call to action for our time."
KATHRYN GOETZKE
CEO of The Mood Factory
Founder of iFRED
International Advocate of Mental Health

"To become a revolutionary leader, building your EmotionalGRIT is the new metric of success for business leaders, teachers, coaches, and students alike. Without it- you cannot thrive."
AJIT NAWALKHA
Co-founder Mindvalley
CEO Evercoach

"Shifting your perspective to push humanity forward, is what the world needs more of- this book aims to challenge that."
GABRIEL BALDINUCCI
Chief Strategy Officer, Singularity University

"Calling all entrepreneurs, get your EmotionalGRIT on! Finally, a brilliant piece that highlights what it takes to be a revolutionary leader combining behavioral, brain science, and positive psychology to make it easier to incorporate for your teams, families, and your life."

ALEX ECHOLS
Serial Entrepreneur
Top 30 under 30 influencer
Best-Selling Author

"Emotional GRIT creates a platform where compassion and empathy is at our core in problem-solving and building better communities, closer families, and stronger relationships."

NOVALENA J. BETANCOURT
CEO & Author, The Total Female Package

"Millennials are in need of connection, purpose and curiosity. Emotional GRIT redefines what it looks like in every aspect of your life."

YASMINE EL BAGGARI
Founder of Voyaj
Recipient of Forbes 30 under 30 Award

EMOTIONAL

GRIT

8 Steps to Master Your Emotions,
Transform Your Thoughts, and
Change Your World

Dr. Neeta Bhushan

EMOTIONAL GRIT
8 Steps to Master Your Emotions, Transform Your Thoughts, and Change Your World

EmotionalGRIT.com
Info@emotionalgrit.com

Ordering Information:
Quantity sales. Special discounts are available on quantity purchases by corporations, associations, and others. For details, contact the "Special Sales Department" with the Publisher at the email address above and type in subject line "Special Sales Department."

The views expressed in this work are solely those of the author and do not necessarily reflect the views of the publisher, and the publisher hereby disclaims any responsibility for them.

Cover design by Angela Kung
Book design by Storehouse Publishing, LLC
Internal graphics design by Krysta Francoeur
Editing by Ally Machete & Team, Michelle Herrera, Kate-Madonna Hindes
Author photograph by Naomi Chu

EMOTIONAL GRIT / Dr. Neeta Bhushan. —1st ed.

ISBN: 978-0-9977675-2-0 (sc)
ISBN: 978-0-9977675-3-7 (ebk)

Library of Congress Control Number: 2016952440

Printed in the United States of America

TABLE OF CONTENTS

Introduction
Change Your Life, Change Your World   9

PART ONE: A Call for More Compassion and Empathy   19
Chapter 1: Human Disconnection—The Dilemma of Today's
World   21
Chapter 2: Human Drivers of Success and a Cry for New
Leadership   31
Chapter 3: Get Ready to GRIT   47

PART TWO: **GROW**. Reveal. Innovate. Transform.
Grow —Becoming *Aware* of Your World   61
Chapter 4: The Road to Self-Mastery—Connecting Past
Stories Along the Way   65
Chapter 5: The EmotionalGRIT Kit—Using Empathy Tools
to Nail the Emotions Game   87

PART THREE: Grow. **REVEAL**. Innovate. Transform.
Reveal—To *Accept the Past is to Move Forward*   109
Chapter 6: Having Courage to Feel Fear   113
Chapter 7: Your Boundaries Vs. Boundless Curiosity   133
Chapter 8: Who Is In Charge? You or Your Ego?   159
Chapter 9: Forgive, Let Go, and Redefine Your Identity   185

PART FOUR: Grow. Reveal. **INNOVATE**. Transform.
Innovate—The *Commitment* to Change   203
Chapter 10: Emotional Flexibility to Innovate   207
Chapter 11: GRATITOOLS: A Toolbox Loaded with a New
Perception and Perspective   223

PART FIVE: Grow. Reveal. Innovate. **TRANSFORM**.
Transform—Take Responsibility and Take *Action*   235
Chapter 12: Elevate Your Life with New Anchors   239
Chapter 13: Leaders: Get Ready to Change Your World   259
Chapter 14: Hacking Your Revolutionary Human Potential   269

****

Acknowledgements	281
Your EmotionalGRIT Kit	283
Resources	285
Key Characteristics	287
EmotionalGRIT Suite	291
End Notes	293
About the Author	299

INTRODUCTION

CHANGE YOUR LIFE, CHANGE YOUR WORLD

I had an epiphany many years ago. You might call it an awakening or rebirth. Something inside me just said, "This, this is your opportunity to invest time in yourself now."

Growing up in a Filipino-Indian household with traditional Asian "tiger" parents meant, as has now been made famous by a bestselling book, that I had to always portray an image of near-perfection and educational success. These ideals were crucial for my family to show others that we were good and worthy—that I was a good and worthy daughter.

The façade would come crumbling down a few years later, when, as a teenager, I lost both of my parents and my brother each to debilitating disease. I then got married and after realizing that the drive forced into my brain and soul from an early age—that outward show that all is oh-so-perfect—continued into my marriage, ruling it and ruining it and me. I ended that unhappy marriage, experiencing a complete upheaval in everything I thought to be fixed, true, and perhaps permanent. This storm shook me to my core and as the last leaves left my branches, stripped of all falsehoods and pretense, I finally understood who I was—and am to this day.

Forced to now play the hand I was dealt, I embarked on my own personal journey of self-discovery and emotional endurance and for the first time, lived and thought outside of society's ideas and ideals of "perfection."

Coming from—this traditional background, as I grew up it was culturally taboo to share feelings or to challenge and question 'the box,' let alone think outside of it. While on the one hand, spiritual inquiry was encouraged in my home (my mom was Catholic and my father Hindu), the strict expectations of obligatory obedience and cultural subordination left me with a particular story I had to tell, especially as the first-born woman in the house. I was encouraged to fall in line with the status quo. This meant people pleasing, family pleasing, legacy building, image maintaining, pride upholding and more. Though I didn't realize it at the time, being confined within this–small "box" of others' expectations, I was on the fast track to either burst or burnout.

Fueled by an inner resilience, and having gone through many inner struggles-turned-dialogues, I've arrived at a definitive, self-leadership framework centered around authenticity, vulnerability, and ultimately, owning your old stories and being committed to authoring your new ones. I call it EmotionalGRIT.

EmotionalGRIT: Grow, Reveal, Innovate, and Transform— The Journey

In the coming pages, I'll lay out a path for your own journey of transformation and offer you advice on how to break out of a box you may be in, whether due to expectation, cultural norms, or even the sense of being comfortable but not fully alive. I'd like to help you shed light on how you can regain your sense of self and the integrity to do your greatest work in this life. Otherwise, living the way you are now may only lead to burnout, angst, and disease, thus perpetuating the never-ending cycle of an unfulfilled life.

Allow me to go back to the turning point in my life when I was hiding within the shame of my own internal story. I was deemed traditionally successful on the outside: the perfect marriage, the ambitious couple, and the glamour of being the quintessential "model" for other young doctors beginning their journey. Younger than thirty, reaching the pinnacle of high-drive, overarching success, we had a dazzling six-figure Bollywood wedding, the million-dollar dream home, and a first-class travel style.

Yet, inside I was crumbling. I was living a lie, scared to death of my actual situation. I was in a physically and emotionally abusive marriage, living in fear, and even more fearful of what the world would think of me. I was so fearful of what society would think if they knew the truth: that I was a complete fraud. Would I be judged? Would I be accepted by my colleagues, my family and friends, and the community that I served? Would I be worthy and noble in society after losing my parents and brother before I was nineteen?–Marriage was the ticket for safety in society, or at least that's what I thought at that point. I thought my image-conscious life wasn't perfect enough as a cosmetic dentist with a high-profile clientele of executives and CEOs.

Yet my real life at that point was so filled with violence, perpetuated by ego, and fueled by the external show of pleasing everyone that it even seeped into how I lead my business partnerships and dealt with my employees and even my patients, all through the perception of fear.

In understanding my "old" story, the quest for self-discovery and the path to self-mastery emerged from the beautiful lesson often hidden in life's greatest adversities. As life happens *for* you and not *to* you, it's the points of resilience that test the core of your values and your beliefs—and reveal your inner strength. That journey is what I now call GRIT. Grow, Reveal, Innovate, and Transform.

In its simplest form, that's exactly what I did. After filing for divorce, and enduring the trials of deep pain in separation, the cloud of pain began to lift. I found much solace in the fact that for the first time in my life, I began my quest to build up my internal strength. Filling my cup first, and allowing myself the permission to be "selfish," whereas culturally a Filipino-Indian, I sacrificed my happiness for the sake of family, society, and others. In the years that would follow on my quest for self-discovery and traveling around the world, I sold my dental practice, moved to San Francisco, and began championing and speaking globally about emotional strength intelligence for a new era of leadership.

There is a certain bravado required to question the traditional norms and lead from a different lens; to truly question the decisions that you make and the fundamental reasons behind them. The social-emotional awareness we possess and how our emotions affect our decision-making process as leaders is one of the main lessons in the school of life.

> There is a certain bravado required to question the traditional norms and lead from a different lens; to truly question the decisions that you make and the fundamental reasons behind them.

Now that I fully understand the human dynamics and behavioral psychology of different types of leaders, I see that I had to go through it all to bring together this foundation in order for me to develop the core concepts of GRIT—and to be able to explain GRIT so that you can adopt it into your own life.

I immersed myself in growth opportunities of every kind, merging different worlds and learning from different schools of thought. I hunted through 45-plus countries to understand the varying perspectives of true global and human stories of transformation, adversity, and awareness. I have now merged psycho-emotional behavior dynamics and brain science with stories of emotional intelligence to inspire a mandatory change in our collective mindset and provide you with a new approach to your life.

> To achieve authentic happiness, you must first uncover what stories are playing out in your life.

So, to encourage a new framework of thinking, what about starting with honoring the reasons behind the decisions we make? It is time to question your belief systems and spark a revolution of curiosity to shift your current pattern of solving problems in your own micro-sphere. Instead of leading with the mask we sometimes wear, I encourage you to remove it once and for all to reveal a different face that is beyond the stories that are part of the past to reach a new frontier, built on action and the courage to rise tall despite the things that once happened *to* you.

New solutions are on the horizon. We must be champions of our stories and build an internal foundation so solidly grounded in authentic living that it spills over into the entire life you choose to lead.

Let go of the fear of disappointing and not belonging and rise to the new call of solidarity and collaboration, creating a more humanistic, connected and heart-centered society as a result.

I will speak in the coming pages a great deal about leadership. While I do often mean it in the context of the workplace, it can extend to self-leadership to conduct your own life in a new and directed way, free of old habits and energized by a new vision.

EmotionalGRIT establishes a new model of human leadership within and beyond the workforce—to build a more heart-centered, compassionate environment in companies, communities, schools, and families—so that you can master your inner strength and positively impact the world around you. To achieve authentic happiness, you must first uncover what stories are playing out in your life.

> Self-leadership to conduct your own life in a new and directed way, free of old habits and energized by a new vision.

I hope you're ready to ride this wave—the wave that is EmotionalGRIT: Grow, Reveal, Innovate, and Transform—because it's time for an emotional revolution.

<u>When reading this book, I suggest keeping a couple of things handy:</u>

- Materials for notes: These include a notebook and pen. (While there is an area after each chapter to take notes, you may find you need more space). At the end of the book, I'll ask you to share your GRIT transformation with others and me in our online community. You'll need to rely on those notes to piece it together.
- An open mind: You're likely going to experience a myriad of emotions while going through this book and its exercises. Allow time for reflection and time for implementation in your daily routine. The EmotionalGRIT workbook is an additional resource you can use to keep yourself on track with your goals.

> EmotionalGRIT establishes a new model of human leadership within and beyond the workforce to build a more heart-centered, compassionate environment in companies, communities, schools, and families—so that you can master your inner strength and positively impact the world around you.

Here is a poem or mantra that summarizes the journey of EmotionalGRIT, and you may want to bookmark this page:

When you **grow**, you are more aware.

When you are more aware, you are ready to **reveal**.

When you reveal a better version of yourself, you **innovate**.

When you innovate, you are committing to action.

When you take action, you **transform**.

We are igniting a revolution in your current mindset.

Own your stories, shift your mind, and redefine how you lead your life.

PART 1

A CALL FOR MORE COMPASSION AND EMPATHY

CHAPTER ONE

HUMAN CONNECTION –
THE DILEMMA OF
TODAY'S WORLD

"Pain can break us or make us wiser."
– Eric Reitans, former Navy Seal

Chapter Intention: I will think of each new day as a revolutionary step towards my new future. Today, I'm learning that to become a better leader, I must become a courageous learner. I have all the tools I need and I am curious and ready to grow.

Chapter Checklist

- To become the best leader you can be, you need to examine your life at its core: How do you react in times of stress and what motivates your decisions?
- Have you ever experienced stress, anxiety or depression? I believe, as do many others, that many causes of these human conditions stem from a lack of self-awareness and debilitating fear.
- Do you feel you are truly meeting ALL your needs: Emotional, Physical, Spiritual, And Psychological?

At one time, I was convinced I had it all. With a prosperous dental practice, an outwardly successful marriage, and a gorgeous home, I truly believed I had it all. What separated my future success from my past failure was only one thing—ME—and my inner dialogue that I wasn't enough, that I had to consistently do more. This voice said that I was not ever doing enough and the constant need to overachieve and overdo to gain "acceptance" or "self-worth" from my achievements was constant.

Understanding and becoming more self-aware of my cultural background and the landscape of my upbringing added more complexities to my life, and I've learned to embrace them fully.

So much fear-based leadership runs through our veins in the western world, and now, our current state of worldly affairs only breeds more separation, bigotry and violence.

In my life as a former healthcare professional and cosmetic dentist, during the ten years of work plus my training to be a doctor, I experienced fear-based leadership first hand. My fellow doctors and I were "validated" only by our memorization skills and our right answers, and of course, deathly afraid and conditioned not to make mistakes or have our facts incorrect. Ultimately, this mode of fear-based training both drove our egos sky-high—and left our emotional awareness buried deep inside.

To be taught to think and learn from a given set of rigid principles only serves to fuel the machine of external attachments such as monetary gain, accolades, and awards. Human dynamics and the "why" behind the lessons isn't something often taught or explored. We are driven to earn the approval from our families and worry what society will think. Further perpetuating the school-validation culture, the "smarter" you sound, the better you fit in the "box" and the more boasting you can do for the sake of gaining recognition, acceptance, and credibility. Thus, we become a great "win" for our parents and teachers and live our lives for the sake of their approval.

But *who* are you living your life for? For yourself, or to appease others?

While there is nothing wrong with this approach, the real question becomes, what kind of leadership do you want to govern your own life? Are you willing to reassess and understand what drives your decision making?

In many ways, I'm the same individual I was when I was a youth; I have the same name and the same face. What is drastically different now is my internal grit, or EmotionalGRIT as I've come to describe it. Truthfully, walking away from everything that I thought epitomized success led me to an awakening and internal strength I could ever have imagined. My EmotionalGRIT journey taught me courage and has opened my mind up to so many new possibilities, including a burning desire to share what I've learned with you.

With today's fast-paced distractions, lists, agendas, and the seeming urgency to pile on more, disconnection seems to grow proportionately, dividing, separating and causing large gaps in the workplace, in communities, and at home. The result? A spiral of more stress, anxiety, unhappiness, and unfulfilled dreams. We're all emotionally, physically, and spiritually fatigued.

Due to the lack of time, resources, and energy, businesses and leaders that should take a step back and analyze their core cultures and processes instead plunge ahead to keep up with the demands of this new era, leaving too many unhappy people in their wake.

> # PROBLEM:
> COMPANIES, COMMUNITIES, AND SOME CULTURES HAVE MOVED AWAY FROM THE CORE FOUNDATIONAL PRINCIPLES THAT CONNECT US AS HUMANS.

Stress and Disease

Thomas Insel, the former director of the National Institutes of Health, has stated that we as a population are experiencing a dramatic increase in the rise of psychiatric and mental health related illnesses.

Adrenal failure, anti-anxiety medication, and cancer are at an all-time high. More than ever before, even with all of our medical technologies and advancements, we are continuously distracting ourselves through food, to-do lists, addictions, and more. An obsession with material things has largely replaced independent thought and relationships. Remember, I was once in the same race. I truly believed that my million-dollar home, practice, and husband would bring me happiness. The only thing it brought was self-doubt and stress because my internal world didn't match my exterior facade. Money made nothing better and the only time I was able to look at myself in the mirror and begin to see real worth was when I took my life in my own hands to create something that was all my own.

There's no time for self-reflection in a race where the ultimate goal is to have and do it all. One cannot. Stress management in our daily lives has become mandatory to combat the external pressures of this shifting society. When we bury emotions, it has profound effects on every level of our mind, body, and soul, and especially, as we are learning, even at the cellular level, manifesting in time as disease.

Studies have linked our modern day cancers to neglecting our emotional states. You can, I'm sure, understand that this subject of ill health is very dear to me, given that I lost my parents and a younger brother to diseases within a span of four years in my adolescence. I've become an advocate for emotional strength and emotional health as a result.

> Stress management in our daily lives has become mandatory to combat the external pressures of this shifting society. When we bury emotions, it has profound effects on every level of our mind, body, and soul, and especially, as we are learning, even at the cellular level, manifesting in time as disease.

A whopping 80% of today's diseases are related to stress.

Emerging wellness practices, new alternative and integrative medical mindsets, and ancient Eastern philosophies of mindfulness, stillness, meditation, and yoga are now being brought to the cultural forefront in waves. This myriad of life tools can help everyone cultivate a proper understanding of emotional intelligence, becoming the pivotal first step in noticing your stress-induced state—and increasing your self-awareness, overall health, and your process for making life decisions.

According to the U.S. National Library of Medicine, while not all stress has a negative effect, studies have shown that short-term stress boosted the immune system and that chronic stress had a significant counter effect, ultimately manifesting in the body as illness:

> *"(Stress) raises catecholamine and suppressor T cells levels, which decreases the immune system function. This suppression, in turn raises the risk of viral infection. Stress also leads to the release of histamine, which can trigger severe broncho-constriction in asthmatics. Stress increases the risk for diabetes mellitus, especially in overweight individuals, since psychological stress alters insulin needs. Stress also alters the acid concentration in the stomach, which can lead to peptic ulcers, stress ulcers or ulcerative colitis. Chronic stress can also lead to plaque buildup in the arteries (atherosclerosis), especially if combined with a high-fat diet and sedentary living."*[1]

Stress doesn't just affect you physically; it alters your mental state, making you more vulnerable to depression, nervous behavior, and a low sense of self-worth. What we need instead is a healthy, enlightened state that gives our natural full range of feelings, both positive and negative, a respectful and safe place to be processed, and worked through.

About antidepressants

Famous psychologist Abraham Maslow believed that many mental illnesses were, "Related to spiritual disorders, to loss of meaning, to doubts about the goals of life." But we now know that most mental illnesses are due to a chemical imbalance in the brain and are classified as disease, not disorders. However, I believe that between antidepressants and Maslow's thinking lies a gap; if we looked hard enough, we may be able to see a direct correlation between unmet psychological or emotional needs with levels of stress and depression.

The Mayo Clinic cites that unresolved issues of stress can lead to depression in some individuals:

> *"Chronic stressful life situations can increase the risk of developing depression if you aren't coping with the stress well. There's also increasing evidence of links among poor coping, stress and physical illness."*[2]

The rise in individuals (specifically Americans and the western world) on antidepressants has been called "astounding" by Harvard Medical School. According to a Harvard article from October 2011 reporting on a study by the National Center for Health Statistics (NCHS), the following is true:

- 23% of women in their 40s and 50s take antidepressants, a higher percentage than any other group (by age or sex)
- Women are 2 ½ times more likely to be taking an antidepressant than men
- Less than 1/3 of Americans who are on a single antidepressant (as opposed to several) have seen a mental health professional in the past year

In fact, according to the NCHS report, the rate of teens and adults using antidepressants in the U.S. increased by almost 400% between studies conducted between 1988–1994 and 2005-2008. This increase could be even higher, as I believe that many individuals with depression have gone undiagnosed with a continuing stigma around mental illness, and I also believe that due to marketing and the pharmaceutical industry's agenda, depression has become a very large and lucrative commodity.

I believe to my very core that there is an answer to our dependence on drugs, that there is a better way to fulfillment and happiness, and that is the journey of EmotionalGRIT: Grow, Reveal, Innovate, and Transform.

Read on.

CHAPTER TWO

HUMAN DRIVERS OF SUCCESS AND A CRY FOR NEW LEADERSHIP

"There's much more that unites us than divides us."
– Hillary Clinton

Chapter Intention: I live unapologetically the way that I want and don't take it personally if others don't like it. I make an effort to eliminate and reduce the following negative environments that bring me down: including people, things, thoughts, attitudes and beliefs.

Chapter Checklist

- What is Empathy-Based Leadership?
- How do you understand "your story"?
- What are the human drivers to achieving success?

PROBLEM:
FEAR-BASED LEADERSHIP HAS CAUSED A DIVIDE IN HOW WE APPROACH PROBLEM SOLVING IN OUR HUMAN LEADERSHIP. EMPATHY-BASED LEADERSHIP IS THE ANSWER.

A New Way of Leading: Empathy-Based Leadership

The pressure and weight society places on us conditions all of us— and leaders—to be less authentic. Business leaders often act from a place of what the general public wants instead of what it needs, thus creating a society of unfulfilled worker bees. Instead, we need a heart-centered approach to being human.

The keys to understanding our own human potential lie in the foundation and framework of how our core needs are being met.

Empathy is one of your most powerful tools in this discussion. Empathy is the ability to identify with the feelings and motives surrounding another individual's choices. Empathy is our capacity to recognize the concerns and emotions of others *and* being able to fully understand and accept another person's perspective or decision about a particular situation or lifestyle.

I have some insights and background information on how you can master your trust building, influence, and effective communication, resulting in creating a community of empathetic leaders.

INC magazine published a powerful piece by John Baldoni, which examined the improvements within an organization when empathy is a core focus, without allowing empathy to replace the "toughness" that all leaders must also have. While leaders must be strong motivators of their teams, these same individuals must practice empathy and grace, allowing each person on their team to excel.

> The keys to understanding our own human potential lie in the foundation and framework of how our core needs are being met.

Emotions in the Workplace

Traditionally, the workplace has been associated with hard work, ambition, determination, tough business decisions, cash flow, and profits. Managers and leaders in the business world believed that putting pressure on workers improved performance and brought in greater profits. This business truth is slowly changing as leaders and teams embrace the strength of empathy, putting in place a framework for more collaboration and happier co-workers.

In the new business environment, softer human qualities like empathy and compassion have become not just important but necessary for the performance, growth, and benefit of both individuals and the organization. Empathy and compassion are now seen to be at the core of supportive, productive, meaningful, and favorable relationships that foster the development and progress of better business practices and success.

Showing empathy and compassion in the workplace requires work and a certain mindset. By understanding and caring for others, you develop strong, healthy, and close relationships, helping the team to work together efficiently and being able to create a non-judgmental and accepting culture.

How does empathy affect your interpersonal relationships?

- Understanding the roots of behavior is key. The psychology of behavior and behavior dynamics science tells us that 90% of the way you are at work, in leadership, and in relationship to partnerships is a direct result of how you wanted to be perceived by your parents as a child.
- Understanding your loved ones as a leader of your home, with your friends, significant others, and families allows you to not take things personally. It is so important to see things from their perspective and acknowledge their feelings. Later on in the book, we will get into more specifics around this.

How do you show empathy and compassion in your place of work?

- Listen to what individuals say with an open mind and without interrupting. Practice active listening and pay attention to their body language. Try to understand their feelings and emotions. By taking care in communication, it demonstrates that you value and respect what others say and feel. This allows your peers to come to you first with issues or opportunities.

- Offer support on personal issues. Inquire about your team's personal life—and do so with genuine curiosity. Include families in informal company events, creating a culture of inclusion and acceptance. By taking an interest in your team member's family, you're saying, "I truly care about what is important to you."
- Greet others by name to create a feeling of acceptance and bonding. Assure them that you are always available for advice or even an informal conversation. Show clearly that you value them as individuals.
- Show your empathy through body language: maintain eye contact and let your body posture show openness. Help them understand the reasons for poor performance and enable them to improve and excel.
- Smile at people. Show appreciation in order to encourage others.
- Create a place of warmth and inclusion in meetings. Call out those by name that are quieter or are holding back, or meet with them before the meeting to offer guidance and encouragement. Help individuals feel more comfortable in speaking up.

Choosing to embrace a culture of compassion and empathy in your organization is a matter of choice: your desire to choose to care, to trust, to understand, to sharpen your people skills and to bridge gaps across countries, cultures, personality types, ethnicities, and socio-economic differences.

Empathy and Profits

Companies that exhibit empathy in their cultures do far better as a result.

According to the World Economic Forum, the ten most empathetic companies allowed their empathy to lead to success. Empathy is not merely a soft skill, "but an urgently needed quality, and one that can contribute to commercial potential," the Forum explained. What did the top ten companies all have in common? They led with empathy in eight key areas. I chose three relevant areas for you to consider when examining your company or leadership role.

1. Do you truly care? The World Economic Forum cited these statistics: "71% of millennials want their colleagues to be like a 'second family'", and "75% feel that the organization should mentor and nurture their talent." Care isn't just for millennials. Companies that practice a healthy work culture experience better-engaged employees who stay longer and recommend the company to others.

> **Shining Example:** Though not on the list of the ten best, Zappos routinely is cited for their commitment to employees' well-being and happiness. Tony Hsieh, CEO of Zappos, believes that by retaining a strong cultural commitment to customer service and internal employees' happiness, employees become advocates and customers become valuable assets in word-of-mouth marketing.

2. Transparency is key. Companies that practice authentic leadership and focus on being transparent with employees and investors fare better during downtimes and develop advocates within the walls of the organization and outside the doors as well. With transparency comes a dedicated internal practice of equity: making sure diversity in hiring brings all genders and races into ranks of leadership, as well as diversity of thought, making all employees feel they have a platform to voice concerns and compliments.

This practice shines outside the company as well, making investors and customers feel like they are being listened to and treated with respect and intelligence.

> **Shining Example:** Whole Foods, which ranked within the top five in the World Economic Forum's Empathy Index, is known for transparency in product labeling. CEO Walter E Robb has been a vocal advocate for open and clear labeling for years.

3. Active listening creates positive conversations. Brands that are empathy-based actively listen not just to employees, but to those who are angry or frustrated with their experience with the brand. The World Economic Forum eloquently explains: "Instead of treating customer complaints as a threat, look upon these extremes as a source of emotional insight for your company. Any form of feedback (even an angry complaint) is a gift. Companies must find ways to listen and learn from feedback, however uncomfortable they make us feel."

> **Shining Example:** Microsoft (who gained a score of 100% on the index) is cited often in the technology community as truly listening to gamers and advocates of the brand, even when costing the company money. Microsoft has solidified their stance by making sure customers feel heard and appreciated.

Does your company culture encourage solution seeking, open dialogue for progressive strategies and innovative ideas?

The Hierarchy of Human Needs

The male gender takes the brunt of jokes for revealing or speaking about feelings in our society and often women also receive negative feedback for sharing or processing feelings. To me, that's absolutely unacceptable. To become a person of true EmotionalGRIT, we must recognize the importance of understanding, owning and processing ALL our feelings, even ones that seem out of place or mundane, or those that are often very difficult to address. I believe when discussing the importance of processing feelings, we need to look at our basic human needs.

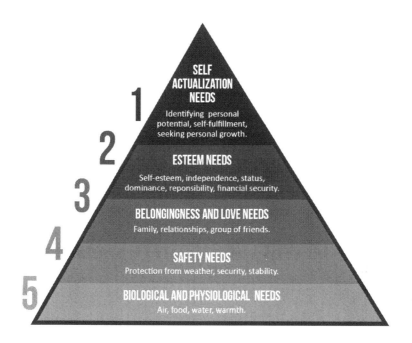

First level – Biological and Physiological needs: Air, food, water, warmth…

Second level – Safety needs: Protection from weather, security, stability…

Third level – Belongingness and Love needs: Family, relationships, group of friends…

Fourth level – Esteem needs: Self-esteem, independence, status, dominance, responsibility, financial security…

Fifth level – Self-Actualization needs: Identifying personal potential, self-fulfillment, seeking personal growth and self-mastery….

In looking at Maslow's hierarchy of needs, I've always noticed a few interesting points:

• Most of us have access to the first three levels, but struggle with the fourth and fifth. I believe that's because while it's accepted in our culture and believed that we must eat, drink, sleep and have family and friends, we rarely discuss our own self-discovery and emotional leadership of our closest relationships.

- Many of us operate out of deeply divided family systems, where we are taught from birth that our best is not "good enough" and therefore we spend a majority of our life trying to live by unreasonable standards. When this happens, it's near-impossible to fulfill the fifth level needs because we are still busy trying to attain the third and fourth.
- Personal growth has become such a hot topic while being so widely misunderstood. To be good leaders, parents, coworkers, and human beings, we must always acknowledge the importance of striving to better *ourselves* before we better those around us.

This idea of emotional leadership is a call for our time. If we have emotions that we haven't reconciled, we truly cannot meet each of the five levels of needs in our own lives. I believe this is directly tied to high suicide rates in the overachieving, overdoing, and tremendous pressure we bury on ourselves to in the art of attaining. Could not achieving our needs be causing a chemical imbalance in our brains and bodies?

> *"Human life will never be understood unless its highest aspirations are taken into account. Growth, self-actualization, the striving toward health, the quest for identity and autonomy, the yearning for excellence (and other ways of phrasing the striving "upward") must by now be accepted beyond question as a widespread and perhaps universal human tendency"* … (Maslow, 1954, Motivation and Personality, pp.xii-xiii)

Understanding Our Needs

The following shape the basic understanding of our decision-making process, and at the very basic level what we desire at the core needs as humans:

- appreciation
- enough-ness
- validation
- worthiness
- inclusion/belonging

To understand why we are the way we are, we need to first comprehend our brain functions and its ties to emotional intelligence. While this may sound scientific and long-winded, it's actually fascinating! When we process an experience, whether joy or loss, our brain imprints the experience into our entire body. Put non-scientifically, as children we learned not to touch something too hot or too cold because the consequence was discomfort or pain. The physical act of being uncomfortable or experiencing pain imprinted itself into our brain and acted as a reminder. This is the same for emotionally painful experiences. If we were taught that our efforts were not worthy, or that our moments of success didn't resonate with our parents, we would begin to deeply doubt who we are and what we bring to the table.

Study after study has been conducted on the importance of healthy relationships with others and a sense of positive self-worth. Like the old adage that we are what we eat, we are also what we think and believe.

To start to unleash your inner GRIT, we must first look at:

- How stress affects the brain.
- The hierarchy of human needs.
- How we process moments of pain and loss.

Everything in your life is shaped by your emotional health. And your "internal belief system" dictates your perceived worth. While not all of our belief systems align, we all have a set of "moral codes" we live by. One person may find deep fault or guilt in over-eating, while another finds it perfectly acceptable. Even universal truths are different, depending on whom you may ask.

The point is that our emotional strength and our emotional fitness arises from our state of mind and our ability to make better, conscientious decisions in our lives when we are more aware—and have experienced the GRIT journey. This is one reason I'm such a vocal advocate for teaching GRIT not only to adults but those in school. Every human being needs to be able to process emotions and learn tools to master the feelings that show up in our everyday lives. This skill set is pivotal to our success as leaders, parents, family members, professionals, friends and more.

Understanding the human emotions of change, grief, and loss

With loss or pain in our lives, it is like we are waking up every day to struggle through invisible emotional pain. It affects our lives as parents, leaders, family amounts of pain points and friends, but it doesn't have to. The fact is every single human being has experienced change or negativity around change in their lives— whether grief, or loss or confusion, adversity and pain affect us all.

> "*When life sucks you under, you can kick against the bottom, break the surface, and breathe again. You choose. It is the hard days — the times that challenge you to your very core — that will determine who you are. You will be defined not just by what you achieve, but by how you survive.*" – Sheryl Sandberg, COO of Facebook and bestselling author

In sharing openly about the sudden and tragic loss of her husband, Sheryl Sandberg has contributed to fully understanding and processing some of life's tribulations.

To recognize our displaced negative emotions, we must look to why we struggle so hard to push them away. We distract ourselves with everything external to numb the pain: food, sex, alcohol, shopping, busyness, and even creating obstacles for yourself to avoid confronting your pain.

Emotions that are not inherently positive are often seen as weakness, especially in Western society. I believe we deeply struggle to recognize our own feelings and apply our emotional intelligence to each emotion because we lack proper support systems and guidance.

To become our most true selves, we must recognize what life events have shaped and molded us into the individuals we are at this moment. I believe that only then, can we become the leaders we are meant to be.

Having lost three members of my immediate family over a span of four years during my adolescence tested the core of my strength, but it also taught me profound resilience, compassion, and impermanence before I was 20. Every year, right before Christmas, I celebrate the memory of my late parents and brother and know their essence is always around, especially in the families and friends I have been grateful to feel welcomed by around the world.

> We distract ourselves with everything external to numb the pain: food, sex, alcohol, shopping, busyness, and even creating obstacles for yourself to avoid confronting your pain.

For those of you experiencing deep pain from loss, adversity, or setback, may you find the strength within. It takes courage, intention, commitment, and discipline to give yourself permission to go through the process.

Here are five tips for utilizing adversity and pain as a direction in your daily life:

1. **Trust and Surrender.** Take the time to feel, mourn and experience all the emotions of grief. But then, slowly and ever-so-carefully . . . *let go*.
2. **Surround yourself with positive daily messages and reminders.** From cards to magazine pictures and clippings, fill your surroundings with images and words that inspire your confidence and enrich your soul.
3. **Practice being truly grateful.** Every day, start with five items you are grateful for. Remember that simply waking up is something that's an incredible gift. Recognize the small and wonderful items that make up your daily life: warm coffee, great friends, and quiet evenings.
4. **Have faith.** Surround yourself with a loving community with or without religion. Find like-minded individuals that give their love before they ask for anything in return and never, ever doubt what an important and magnificent human being you are.
5. **Take proactive care of your mental wellbeing.** We are living in a time where our environment breeds challenges in every avenue of life. Stress management and being proactive is absolutely essential for your daily routine. Seek out therapists, coaches, advisors, or a rock solid community and friends that will actively listen and help you along your process. Grief and allowing yourself to reflect and understand those emotions gives you the opportunity to learn, let go, and move on. By having a sounding board to express yourself, you'll be more apt to flow more evenly and productively through the grief process.

> To become our most true selves, we must recognize what life events have shaped and molded us into the individuals we are at this moment.

Remember that you have the choice to be the architect of your life by working towards becoming the best version of yourself, to reach your new potential, one filled by embracing your EmotionalGRIT journey to true happiness.

5 TIPS TO USE ADVERSITY TO PROPEL YOU FORWARD IN YOUR DAILY LIFE

TRUST AND SURRENDER

Take the time to feel, mourn and experience all the emotions of grief. But then, slowly and ever-so-carefully. . . let go.

SEEK POSITIVITY

Surround yourself with positive daily messages and rminders. From cards to magazine pictures and clippings, fill your surroundings with images and words that inspire your confidence and enrich your soul.

PRACTISE BEING TRULY GRATEFUL

Every day, start with five items you are grateful for. Remember that simply waking up is something that's an incredible gift. Recognize the small and wonderful items that make up your daily life: warm coffee, great friends, and quiet evenings.

HAVE FAITH

Surround yourself with a loving community with or without religion. Find like-minded individuals that give their love before they ask for anything in return and never, ever doubt what an important and magnificent human being you are.

TAKE CARE OF YOUR MENTAL HEALTH

Seek out therapists, coaches, advisors, or a rock solid community and friends that will actively listen and help you along your process. Grief and allowing yourself to reflect and understand those emotions gives you the opportunity to learn, let go, and move on. By having a sounding board to express yourself, you'll be more apt to flow more evenly and productively through the grief process.

CHAPTER THREE

GET READY TO GRIT

"Love and compassion are necessities, not luxuries. Without them, humanity cannot survive." – The Dalai Lama

Chapter Intention: To re-frame my leadership, I must re-frame my chosen actions. Today, I take ownership of my actions and make one decision—to commit to the GRIT journey as an extraordinary human.

The Answer to Leadership's Most Challenging Questions

The previous two chapters laid down the foundation of the challenges we currently face in our shifting world.

Everyone has a story, but more often than not it feels as though we are reading from a pre-written book that's been handed to us rather than creating a beautiful journal and journey that is by our own experience and design.

To be a leader starts with you. You can author your own life, and your story will become the guide, the example for others to awaken their own leadership.

EmotionalGRIT pushes forth a new era of understanding our past stories, using them as fuel to propel our gifts to create a ripple effect in society. Being human centered and heart-centered is at the core of this approach.

Your biggest revolution to-date will be EmotionalGRIT, and here are some of the steps and characteristics of the process.
It is important to understand your emotions through:

- awareness
- acceptance
- commitment
- action

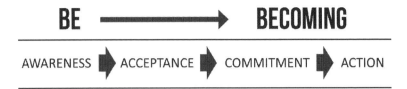

The pioneer of Emotional Intelligence Theory, Daniel Goldman, coined the term "emotional intelligence"—which may be more important than mental IQ.

Emotional intelligence (EI) reflects an individual's potential for mastering the skills of Self-Awareness, Self-Management, Social Awareness, and Relationship Management.

Being emotionally intelligent has begun to show up now in characteristics of emotional management, and even being introduced as forms of empathy and compassion in schools.

Ultimately it comes down to understanding and being aware of our emotions and having a baseline understanding of the emotions we experience on a daily basis.

The most common *positive* emotions you may experience on a daily basis:

- excited
- creative
- happy
- joyous
- empowered
- motivated
- peaceful
- abundant
- inspired
- enthusiastic

The ten most common *negative* emotions you may experience on a daily basis:

- anxious
- sad
- empty
- alone
- alone
- stressed
- insecure
- unconfident
- self-critical
- misunderstood
- incompetent

How have these contributed to the way you lead? In your business, life, relationships?

Guess what. Here's your permission! You don't have to live by your past "stories" or "circumstances" anymore. EmotionalGRIT gives YOU permission to ignite a revolution.

MOST COMMON POSITIVE & NEGATIVE EMOTIONS

POSITIVE EMOTIONAL STATES

compassionate / creative / connected / successful / appreciated / deserving / loving / playful / calm / excited / thoughtful / happy joyous / kind / content / motivated / peaceful / supported / valued inspired / purposeful / enthusiastic / invigorated / friendly / driven empowered / confident / attractive / abundant / limitless / present fulfilled / relaxed

NEGATIVE EMOTIONAL STATES

anxious / sad / empty / alone / numb / insecure / unconfident self-critical / misunderstood / incompetent / isolated / unsupported outcast / hopeless / unloved / worrisome / unattractive / stressed resentful / depressed / jaded / bored / inadequate / inferior frustrated / confused / angry / overwhelmed / unhappy / outdated envious / judged

All humans want to achieve these five things in their lifetime:

- ✓ acceptance
- ✓ worthiness
- ✓ appreciation
- ✓ enough-ness
- ✓ belonging

And I believe to really and truly become and achieve each of these five, we must master **EmotionalGRIT: the journey of the old story, the awareness of the present, and a *shift* to the future**. While often a masculine term or used to describe physical work, I want us to re-frame the word GRIT to mean the following:

Grow. Reveal. Innovate. Transform.

Let's Explore the GRIT Journey

When you **grow**, you are more aware.
When you are more aware, you are ready to **reveal**.
When you reveal a better version of yourself, you **innovate**.
When you innovate, you are committing to action.
When you take action, you **transform**.
We are igniting a revolution in your current mindset.
Own your stories, shift your mind, and redefine how you lead your life.

Quite simply, EmotionalGRIT is a new approach to a changing workplace and lifestyle paradigm. When distractions are more than ever and pressures to perform are endless, mastering emotions matters most at these times, helping you infuse calm and awareness into your personal and professional life. From a leadership standpoint, it is what has differentiated Google as being consistently ranked as the best place to work. It's the reason why bosses are hiring professional coaches and consultants to support their teams beyond the workday grind. Why corporations are beginning to utilize corporate wellness and development to shape a company's culture in order to have more team engagement, happiness, and fulfillment in the workplace. It's the difference between treading corporate water and making a big business splash, allowing for more financial and personal growth.

Here are five ways to start your EmotionalGRIT training to become an even more effective leader:

1. **All great leaders work on their GRIT:** Being nimble and flexible as challenges arise and becoming easily adaptable are essential to strong leadership. Can you think of a time when you were this was tested in this way? What happened as a result?
2. **Identify your happy place:** When faced with a stressful situation, how can you easily tap-into a better emotional state? Maybe it's a favorite song, a scent, or a beautiful picture of your

family, but having a go-to "happy place" can make all the difference in times of turbulence.

3. **Be still and be OKAY with it:** Meditation and guided visualization is helpful in both stressful situations and times of peace. Many of today's most impactful leaders have and incorporate a lifestyle of mindfulness. All it takes is five to ten minutes per day.

4. **Create a consistent morning routine or what I call, "Morning Bliss":** Incorporating a morning routine such as reading or eating a healthy breakfast while speaking affirmations is one way to keep up your physical and mental state. We speak about this in detail in one of the later chapters, and consists of 3-5 simple small things you can do for yourself. Consider having a consistent and well-balanced morning routine to set your entire day right.

5. **Take the time to journal your thoughts:** Putting thoughts into written form can be extremely cathartic. As Shakespeare once said, "Know thyself"; this is important to building your emotional strength.

The Four EmotionalGRIT Steps: A Closer Look.

Grow (Awareness)

- Self-mastery, Self-Belief, Self-Discovery
- Understanding your stories, limiting beliefs that have held you back
- De-mystifying habits and patterns of behavior
- Finding internal purpose and mission

Reveal (Acceptance, Acknowledge, Celebrate)

- Stepping out of fear
- Creating your new story
- Diving into your beliefs and values
- Celebrating your strengths and understanding your shortcomings
- Forgiving your past, letting go, and creating boundaries

Innovate (Commit, Challenge, Change, Redefine)

- Challenging your perspective
- Understanding your ego
- Gaining new perspective

Transform (Action, Strategy, Next steps)

- Understanding purpose
- Elevating your potential
- Building new anchor points and foundations
- Keeping yourself accountable

Key characteristics explored during the GRIT process of extraordinary leadership in cultivating the new era of human potential are as follows:

> **Authenticity**: The ability to fully be yourself no matter what. Expressing the truest form of you, the quirks that make you unique, the strengths of your personality. The shortcomings that you discover about yourself and that you accept anyway. It is the version of yourself that encompasses all of the things that you love without worrying about society, family, friends, or external noise of who you are expected to be.

> **Drive**: If you are going to create lasting value in the world, there are definitely going to be high points and low points. The real question to consider is your tenacity and motivation for perseverance. It is easy to give up and quit when it seems like the universe is crashing down on you. It becomes your responsibility to adapt to the complexities and rise above with determination.

> **Enthusiasm**: Attitude is everything. Think of when you are having a challenging day. Everything just seems to be the absolute worst. Your car broke down, you are running late, you haven't had anything to eat all day, and you are "hangry". When you are leading a team, your family, and your friends, it becomes

your responsibility to change the energy in the room with your enthusiasm—even when you may not be feeling your best.

> **Courage**: The willingness and boldness to speak and share your voice and opinion. To truly take a stance, without the consequence of hurting feelings of others, fully sharing your truth and allowing the bravado to be seen and heard unapologetically.

> **Curiosity**: Leading your life with this characteristic will change your business, personal relationships, love relationships *and* help further a more connected world. There is no judgment in curiosity: the thirst for deeper understanding and the inquisitiveness to know more. To understand why, and to pursue the unknown, gain a different perspective, learn a different thought process, and encourage openness and expansion. This is the top characteristic when surveying over 500 top leaders, executives, futurists, and thinkers.

> **Presence/focus**: Mindfulness, calm, awareness, and peace in the busyness of the lives we currently live in is important to your internal framework. It's your internal foundation and dialogue of peace, neither concerned with the past nor the future and living in each moment fully engaged and connected, that is so powerful. Efficiency and productivity is enhanced when we are focused and can achieve much more in our lives with less mindful clutter.

> **Empathy**: Embracing the new era of the next generation you are leading, being sensitive and open to the feelings of others is vital. Understanding the perception and the perspective of the other person. The reasons behind someone else's decision making and thought process. Kindness and warmth are hallmarks of a new era of leadership.

> **Compassion**: The understanding to have self-compassion, knowing that you are doing the best that you can. Removing the pressures that we sometimes place on ourselves that can cause overdoing, overachieving, and overanalyzing removes anxiety,

manages stress better, and allows for empathy and kindness to shine through. Compassion kindles a more heart-centered approach to solve some of the most challenging and complex problems in our lives.

> **Adaptability**: Being flexible is one of the single most valuable characteristics you can embody to move with the seasons of life. The challenges of the moment, the sometimes unexpected and unexplainable situations that arise that test your core strength. The ability for you to pivot, change direction, shift your mindset, and become fluid with the unexpected is remarkable not only in leadership of life, but more important, to stabilize your internal foundation as well as your influence on others.

> **Vulnerability**: This is one of the single most game-changing characteristics you can make a part of you that will change your world. Traditionally seen as a sign of weakness in some cultures, when you are able to be vulnerable and showcase a more human and relatable side to you, it offers humility, trust, and respect that is welcomed by others. It offers a tremendous opportunity for us to realize we are imperfect beings, to celebrate our flaws and champion some aspects that make us human, which is desperately something we need to create more collaboration and cohesion within families, businesses, communities, and societies.

> **Resilience**: Understanding that adversity is a part of life you need to recognize that it engenders tenacity and a fierce capacity to rise up again and again. It feeds the understanding of the ebb and flow of life. In every single life there will be dark times, and it's not about avoiding them altogether, but rather understanding how to navigate through the challenging aspects of life by embracing some of its toughest pain points. It is not about being the victim; rather it's embracing the valuable lessons that strengthen your core as a human as a result. The key to resilience is seeing the silver lining in each scenario so that you can be stronger as a result.

Here are some institutions that exemplify the incorporation of EmotionalGRIT into their core ethos in building new leadership:

- Stanford's University Center for Care and Compassion Institute founder and neuroscientist Dr. James Doty has linked compassion and kindness as hard-wired in our brains.
- Harvard University's Daniel Goldman, pioneer in emotional intelligence, has defined this as the *sine qua non* of leadership. Without it, a person can have the best training in the world, an incisive, analytical mind, and an endless supply of smart ideas, but she or he still won't make a great leader.
- The Yale Center for Emotional Intelligence highlights the core trait of empathy by infusing it in schools and curriculum to redefine education for the next generation.
- The Dalai Lama Fellows is working to reimagine leadership at the global level with curriculum that empowers young leaders working in 27 countries around the globe.
- Dr. Angela Duckworth's work at UPenn's CharacterLabs investigates GRIT as a core characteristic in shaping behavior to thrive.

Immediate Goals:

- Celebrate your first step. Time to reflect. Have you paid attention to how you show up to your family, friends, colleagues, or significant other? What characteristic sticks out the most in preparing for your EmotionalGRIT? Set aside 10 minutes to write your first few thoughts about the first steps in your emotionalGRIT process.

Recommended reading:

- ***Emotional Intelligence,* by** Martin Seligman
- ***Revolution from Within,* by** Gloria Steinem
- ***Gifts of Leadership:*** Team Building Through Empathy and Focus**, by** Art Horn

- *Primal Leadership: Learning to Lead with Emotional Intelligence,* by Daniel Goleman, Richard E. Boyatzis, Annie McKee
- *Crucial Conversations: Tools for Talking When Stakes Are High,* by Kerry Patterson, Rob McMillan, Al Switzler
- *Drive: The Surprising Truth About What Motivates Us,* by Daniel H. Pink

PART 2

GROW. REVEAL. INNOVATE. TRANSFORM.

GROW
Becoming *Aware* of Your World

"Whatever ceases to grow, begins to die."
– Albert B. Simpson

What allowed the young Kat Cole to grow from being just another Hooters waitress to becoming the president of the billion-dollar company Cinnabon? Her awareness of all the hidden opportunities around her every day. This keen insight allowed her to rise up through the ranks at incredible speed, going from a waitress who was both passionate and patient (making close to double her salary because of tips), to becoming executive vice president of that company at age 26 and being entrusted with overseeing the franchising of the brand. She accomplished this without a college degree, dropping out to allow her this freedom to travel. By age 35 Kat was president of Cinnabon and helped it launch in over 56 countries worldwide.

Kat believes there is greatness in all of us, whether unpolished or not yet realized, it's there. Her high level of EmotionalGRIT has catapulted her career, often doing business in places where it is unheard of for women to be doing business at all. She represents a new era of leadership because she is always focused on the human interaction, therefore drawing out the best in others.

Kat says, *"The domino effect of every human interaction, it goes somewhere. And so if you can be a part of seeing what's possible and helping other people see what's possible…the trajectory that you put the whole world on, is pretty phenomenal."*

The ability to learn a new language, become a better speaker, improve your physical fitness and ultimately realize your potential within society resides in your self-awareness. You have to be fully honest about where you are and how you intend to change your position. Your openness and willingness to own your story directly correlates with the impact you have in this world.

CHAPTER FOUR

THE ROAD TO SELF-MASTERY – CONNECTING PAST STORIES ALONG THE WAY

"Between stimulus and response there is a space. In that space there is our power to choose our response. In our response lies our growth and our freedom." –Victor Frankl

Chapter Intention: Just like a fingerprint, your story is totally and wholly yours. It encompasses your most vulnerable *and* most successful moments. Take time to relish everything you have accomplished, giving yourself grace if you don't yet fully understand your journey. You are on your way!

Chapter Checklist

- Everyone has a few things from their past they would rather leave behind. Can you think of any items from years back that are still causing anxiety or fear?
- We sometimes can be especially hard on ourselves in trying to do more, achieve more, accomplish more, and are often our biggest critiques without even realizing it. How have you shown appreciation and kindness towards yourself in the past week?
- In building your emotional endurance, it takes courage to be honest with yourself, and become aware of the parts of yourself that you love and that need patience. Are you ready to become aware of the culmination of all your life events up until this point?

The first three chapters of this book were all about beginning to understand the EmotionalGRIT process. In the next several pages, we're going to explore the main driver of instilling EmotionalGRIT: You!

As I mentioned, my GRIT journey began years after losing my parents and sibling and walking away from my practice. However, my life journey began at birth. In exploring the GRIT process, I recognized that I needed to acknowledge the items in my past that were causing negative emotions, like fear, regret, and anger. The GRIT process borrows from the old adage that "if it doesn't scare you, it's not worth doing."

You all have stories that may prevent you from becoming aware to the entire picture of your life. Being emotionally aware is simply a large part of this process. Being governed sometimes by how society expects you to think, respond, act for the sake of being 'accepted' can surely place grave limitations on your thought process, and even more so in your decision making.

> The ability to learn a new language, become a better speaker, improve your physical fitness, and ultimately realize your potential within society resides in your self-awareness.

Authenticity in Today's World

Self-mastery is vital to your success inside the office and in your personal and family life. To master your emotions, you need to begin from a place of authenticity, something I feel is truly missing in our educational system and in our world.

Characteristics of extraordinary leaders include being truthful in how you show up in the world. Simply, it is the ability to express your desires, wants, and needs with your unique gifts without worrying about repercussions or "negative" self-talk: "Will I hurt someone's feelings?" "Will I feel bad about being too harsh or disrespectful?" "Will I be non-diplomatic to a point where I put myself in an awkward position?" These are common false concerns for many people, and they prevent them from acting in a way that is authentic in the world.

So how does one go about being authentic or truthful? Before we get into some key exercises, think for a moment: if you stated the true facts about a situation and protected what feels right for you instead of saying what is traditionally expected of you, or giving the standard response that "pleases" everyone around you, you are fair to both yourself and everyone around you. You do the world a disservice if you don't give proper feedback.

> You all have stories that may prevent you from becoming aware to the entire picture of your life.

How can your team members, friends, family members, significant others, and even children grow and become better humans if you are "afraid of hurting feelings" simply because you aren't able to speak your mind and be authentic and truthful? A deeper question is why.

In order to build your authenticity, you need to understand the importance of filling your cup first. This means mastering you.

<u>Here are four reasons why self-mastery is important</u>:

1. Self-mastery helps you make better decisions in response to fully understanding your highest needs and desires.
2. Self-mastery helps you understand and accept the perspective and thinking of others and in return allows you to practice empathetic leadership that comes from a place of mutual respect, awareness, and understanding.
3. Self-mastery leads to cultivating your emotional endurance with EmotionalGRIT so that you are able to develop and nurture a better understanding of yourself, as well as form deeper and more genuine relationships around you.
4. Self-mastery holds you accountable and serves as an internal gauge when you are not being your most authentic self.

This is a fundamental core characteristic of what the world needs more of: truthful, emotionally heart centered humans that can better understand the decision making that arises as a result of when you are more authentic with yourself first. Only then will it begin to create a ripple effect in your business lives, communities, and families that you serve.

The essential component of GROW in the GRIT journey is being open to the awareness behind your decisions. Realizing and understanding the reasons behind the actions is essential. With self-mastery, you begin to cultivate a deeper understanding and self-awareness. This is the secret sauce.

> This is a fundamental core characteristic of what the world needs more of: truthful, emotionally heart centered humans that can better understand the decision making that arises as a result of when you are more authentic with yourself first.

How do our past stories play a role in the workplace?

Boardrooms have their bottom lines, and they are rarely padded with emotional intelligence and empathy-based solutions. When analyzing return on investment, financial growth and employee retention have clear indicators, but can you measure fulfillment and compassion? The *New York Times* published a piece on how schools are measuring emotional skills with students and there was significant backlash.

> *"Argument still rages about whether schools can or should emphasize these skills. Critics say the approach risks blaming the victim — if only students had more resilience, they could rise above generational poverty and neglected schools — and excuses uninspired teaching by telling students it is on them to develop "zest," or enthusiasm. Groups that spent decades urging the country toward higher academic*

standards worry about returning to empty talk of self-esteem, accepting low achievement as long as students feel good."[3]

It may be difficult to do with children, but I measure grit every day with CEOs, executives, and their teams. It's not exactly the same as comparing sales figures from quarter to quarter, but it's not as different as you may think.

For kids, a test in patience may not hold the same weight as a quiz in multiplication. But for working adults in boardrooms and beyond, without grit there is no exponential growth.

Financial growth, employee retention, and most of the hallmarks of successful business are dramatically impacted by the leadership styles of those at the helm. The old model celebrates fear-driven rule, encourages emotionless partnerships, and puts competition before collaboration. In that context, the rougher, the tougher, and the stronger the better. It's an approach that has made our industries prosperous and our nation resilient, but it's an antiquated model for a reason.

Today, corporate wellness, company culture, and employee happiness have taken center stage. Companies across all sectors are enjoying the dynamic benefits that come with investing in individual hearts and minds, not just business-as-usual. After all, many times you spend more time with your teammates than your friends and family, so the idea of fun and creative thinking in the workplace is wildly catching on. Here, the old adage rings true: You get more bees with honey than vinegar. The CEOs and executives I work with find that when they innovate their leadership styles from fear-driven to empathy-based, they are able to tap into new levels of potential within their teams. As a result, they are more receptive to upper management levels when they feel heard, cared for, empowered, and respected—wildly boosting company morale, individual productivity and a greater collective group dynamic.

The results? *Well, they're pretty incredible.*

Steven's story:

I agreed to help Steven, a top tier CEO. Fear ran through his veins. The youngest in a family known for their deeply successful business acumen, it was long thought he would never amount to anything. Even Steven believed he would remain the same child who was labeled a troublemaker, or worse; he was thought of as worthless. So when he started his business, the chip on his shoulder became too much to bear. Steven had a deep desire to prove his self-worth, and more important, his *worthiness*. Steven's fear that he wasn't worthy meant he couldn't, and wouldn't, ask for help. He took everything upon himself, burned out fast, endured health problems, and even depleted his mental and emotional resources.

What if he learned to develop his own level of authenticity as a child? What if he believed his value as an entrepreneur, a son, and a human being wasn't tied to someone else's vision of success? What if he wasn't afraid of letting down his parents, family, and society? What if didn't worry about what was "expected of him"? What if he was truthful with himself and governed with honesty about what he truly wanted, instead of what "looks good" or "should be" to save face? What if he wasn't afraid of being judged and simply had the self-awareness to choose differently?

In Steven's case, we worked together on exercises and scenarios to rewire his brain and redefine his approach to business through empathy and compassion. He went from scrambling for validation to stepping forward with a new framework of thinking simply by shifting his mindset. He learned the importance of self-awareness, how to ask for help and be vulnerable. But most importantly, what it means to be a real leader simply by being human.

We have many CEOs in the world just like Steven. They are holding onto past traumas or challenges from childhood, trying to win the love of their families, fighting the notion that they're simply not good enough. (As the daughter of "tiger parents" who endured a number of family pressures and sold a million-dollar business that wasn't fulfilling her, I should know.) Because most leaders don't have foundations of inner strength and self-discovery, they are unable to make emotional connections with themselves and especially with their teams. Since as leaders, vulnerability is often seen as a sign of weakness, CEOs and leaders like Steve often times will often have a "mask" on never allowing his real shell to shine within the workplace. This is causing debilitating issues for companies, such as broken communication, poor work ethic, misguided leadership, and, in some cases, negative health consequences.

At an early age, we learn how to treat others and ourselves. We want to fit in, and belong to a group: inclusion is the driving force! After all, as humans we yearn for connection. Without a personal foundation of compassion, communication, and understanding, the professional bonds of trust, teamwork, and productivity can never be fully formed. The journey to changing this begins with having a deep awareness and mastery of yourself.

> EmotionalGRIT establishes a new culture of human leadership within and beyond the workforce to build a more heart-centered, compassionate environment in companies, communities, schools and families.

Your authentic self

Popular author and all-around unbelievably talented researcher and speaker Brené Brown had this to say on becoming our true, authentic selves:

> *"When we deny our stories, they define us. When we own our stories, we get to write a brave new ending."*

Much like Brené, I found myself struggling to understand why I was afraid to tell my story of rising above adversity and overcoming loss. I didn't realize I was hiding from my past until the fear of who I was overshadowed my ambition of who I wanted to be. Brené helped me pinpoint each of my own beliefs in her research, and I believe her studies on vulnerability, shame, authenticity and connection have the power to change our society as a whole.

> *"After 15years of social work education, I was sure of one thing: Connection is why we're here; it is what gives purpose and meaning to our lives. The power that connection holds in our lives was confirmed when the main concern about connection emerged as the fear of disconnection; the fear that something we've done or failed to do, something about who we are or where we come from, has made us unlovable and unworthy of connection. I learned that we resolve this concern by understanding our vulnerabilities and cultivating empathy, courage, and compassion—what I call shame resilience."* – Brené Brown

To fully understand ourselves, we must first understand our past. In the previous chapter, we discussed the effects of not letting go of negativity on our emotional health and leadership capability. I believe Brené powerfully points to another element that we often overlook in our GRIT journey: Connection.

EmotionalGRIT establishes a new culture of human leadership within and beyond the workforce to build a more heart-centered, compassionate environment in companies, communities, schools and families.

This allows individuals to master their inner selves and positively impact the world. When we step into the destiny of GRIT, we redefine what it means to have the courage to grow, reveal, innovate and transform into our unrealized potential in humanity. Just like the Velveteen Rabbit, GRIT helps us become the most authentic and powerful version of ourselves.

To be truly authentic, we must hold a connection with every facet of our being. We must engage WHO we are in order to bring valuable personality, unique strengths, and our true selves to the forefront of each day, eliminating personal doubt and fear that who we are is not enough.

> When we step into the destiny of our GRIT, we redefine what it means to have the courage to grow, reveal, innovate and transform into our unrealized potential in humanity.

To understand your authentic self, here are some questions to consider and answer:

- What does real authenticity mean to you?
- How can you speak truth to who you are in each and every moment?
- How often do you wear a "mask" and when does it show up?
- Have you been conditioned be exactly what society expects you 'should' be?
- Can you summarize your life to this point in six adjectives?
- Can you name the top five positive and negative emotions you experience on a daily basis?
- How often do you allow yourself time to reflect on important decisions, emotions, and difficult situations to better understand how your brain connects to your heart? (do you distract yourself with 'things' to avoid reflecting, or are you too busy?)
- Can you pinpoint factors that have motivated you and pushed you to make decisions?

> "We don't see things as they are, we see them as we are." – Anais Nin

Anais Nin's words are such an important reminder that to every challenge we face, we must present our most honest self. We internalize each situation, tinting it with our past experiences and most personal beliefs. Often, we imprint on our work challenges or life challenges, the heavy fear we carry from the past. Authenticity is knowing that fear exists—and choosing to look at the situation in the most confident way possible.

Understanding and Overcoming Fear

Fear creates a sense of urgency that is required, even in small doses, to take action on a project, relationship, or emotion, and I believe the key to overcoming the fear of failure is in strengthening your emotionalGRIT. Despite what you may think about traffic jams, excruciatingly long conference calls, and trials with a tantrum-heavy three year-old, you truly are in control of mastering your emotions. The fact is you can allow your emotions to drive you—or you can be driven by them into a low, pitiful self-loathing energy state where everything feels like failure.

> Fear creates a sense of urgency that is required, even in small doses, to take action on a project, relationship, or emotion, and the key to overcoming the fear of failure is in strengthening your emotionalGRIT.

How do fear and anxiety show up for us as leaders in our own lives?

In understanding the root causes of why we make the decisions we make and become more aware as a result, here is what needs to happen: We need to get a better understanding of the history of fear in the first place.

Daniel Cordero, a professor at the Yale Center of Emotional Intelligence, teaches future leaders about becoming friends with fear and anxiety:

"Fear arises when we experience imminent danger or perceived threat in our environment." He describes that the evolution of fear has become a response to a present danger, whereas anxiety is actually an evolved response to an imagined threat that may occur in the future, which creates stress."

FEAR
PRESENT DANGER

ANXIETY
IMAGINED THREAT THAT MAY OCCUR
IN THE FUTURE, CREATING STRESS

Since we have these pre-conceived stories that we are attached to as far as how fear plays a role in our lives, it begins to form our programming and our process of how we then perceive our "stress" states, therefore holding on to worry, taking less risks, and even more deeply imbedding fear in our brain functions.

From a brain level:

What happens when we experience a negative, or stressful emotional state?

- Our emotional state ----> sends data to the thalamus, our switchboard--->
- Arrives at the amygdala (for reactions) ----> there is a threat
- Automatic sensory response, i.e. stress to the entire body goes off
- Amygdala blocks the slow thinking response to prepare for the anxiety state (flight/fight)
- Shuts down the part of our brain involved in creativity, judgment, and decision-making.

- "perceived anxiety" or "fear" we enter the process of overreacting, overeating, overindulging—or in other words, engage in behaviors to pacify the cycle.

When we can begin to understand some of the fears and perceived anxieties around us, we can begin to dig deeper with the awareness if it truly is a posed threat or if it is one of those "stories" we have replaying in our minds.

Time to check-in! Your turn!

- List some of the fears that you have (fear of not enough time, not good enough, of failure, that you won't have it done on time, that someone will do it better than you, etc.):
- Now, categorize the difference between FEAR and ANXIETY and how it shows up in your life currently (example: I am fearful of spiders, I have anxiety when I have to speak in public):

The science of fear

A big question: how does fear play a role in our decision-making?

Due to the visceral response that fear has over our adrenal system, having us go into a fight/flight mode. Studies have shown that paralyzes our ability profoundly to make good judgments in our behaviors.

- Fearful people tend to make more pessimistic judgments (Lerner & Keltner, 2000).
- Induced fear causes a decreased ability to choose (Luce, 1998)

As a result, many people bury themselves in work, busyness, business, and distractions to achieve success, yet secretly still long for a human connection.

Fear and anxiety in the workplace is an unsightly combo. Whether it's within your teammates or your boss, let this moment be a reminder that you (and only you!) are in control of your actions.

Today, you must make a choice: Will you choose to approach your past with love and compassion, or allow your past to dictate your future success? The choice is yours.

Start out by giving compliments, acknowledgements, and praises through email, written notes, or verbal communications to your team—and don't forget to save some for yourself. You'll begin to influence those around you, and it spreads like wildfire, not only internally, but with your team as well.

WHAT HAPPENS TO YOUR BRAIN DURING FEARFUL EMOTIONAL STATE

OUR EMOTIONAL STATE...

Sends data to the thalamus, our switchboard...

Shuts down the part of our brain involved in creativity, judgment, and decision making. Hence, why our emotions in the presence of "perceived anxiety" or "fear" we enter the process of overreacting, overeating, overindulging—or in other words, engage in behaviors to pacify the cycle.

Arrives at the amygdala (for reactions). If there is a threat...

Automatic sensory response, i.e. stress to the entire body goes off...

Amygdala blocks the slow thinking response to prepare for the anxiety state (flight/fight)

Emotional intelligence overhaul

A few years ago, I uncovered several key factors in how our emotions play a huge role in the workplace. In my deeper investigation in understanding and being fascinated by human dynamics, many of the different stories I collected all shared one alarming trend: a lack of emotional intelligence.

Emotional intelligence is vital to overcome fear and practice authenticity. This is how you manage your emotions when it matters most.

1. **Mastering your EmotionalGRIT helps with efficiency and focus**. When you are emotionally aware and cognizant of the attitudes that you bring to your projects, to your team, and with your workload, you are more likely to stay on-point and not get distracted. This allows you to be fully aware of how to handle difficult conversations, paying attention to your body, mind and soul. Put plainly, mastering your EmotionalGRIT allows you to practice better "gut checks" in the workplace and in your daily life.

2. **Navigating the different personalities in the office**. An emotionally intelligent individual understands that everyone encountered in the workplace has her or his own story, history and personality. Responding to difficult conversations and situations with empathy and compassion signals a highly-emotionally-aware person and creates a "safe space" for others to let their guard down. It's a team builder!

3. **Checking in with yourself, and knowing your boundaries with your boss and team members.** Many CEOs and executives as well as employees have a tough time with boundaries. There's a fine line between taking on too much and saying no. Emotionally aware individuals understand their worth and the importance of self-reflection, allowing for smarter boundaries that create better outcomes.

Here are the true stories of people who took the first steps on their EmotionalGRIT journey through **self-awareness, self-mastery and self-belief**:

"While growing up, the only metric for me of success was wealth and all the symbols of wealth. Coming from humble beginnings and growing up as a poor kid in the sprawling urban landscape of Mumbai, India, I had a keen sense of awareness, and possibility became my main motivation. The biggest turning point for me was when my wife became critically ill, which forced me to adopt a different mindset. Due to various experiences that I have had, I realized that my view was too narrow. Now I live one day at a time. I focus on being mindful in the moment and living it completely. Also whether it's a win or a loss, I know that it's temporary, so I react accordingly. Acting from this place has catapulted my abilities to take my business acumen from the fashion industry exponentially to over 700 brands, with a valuation of over 85 million." Rahul is the CEO of for IndianRoots.com. —Rahul Narvekhar CEO IndianRoots.com

"When I was 15, a young Arab girl from Morocco, I knew I wanted to travel the world. So I set myself a goal that I would do everything I possibly could to live into my dream. In spending a summer with my uncle in San Francisco, the land of possibilities, I knew the US was a place for massive innovation. So, in mastering my self-belief, I was selected by the U.S. State Department to study in the U.S. at 17 years old as a young Moroccan ambassador to encourage Arab women to travel to the US post 9/11. Five years later and traveling to almost all of the 50 states, I've now created the first-ever app that bridges cultural connections with people and common interests. With an emotional IQ algorithm, it matches guests and hosts around the world using shared and authentic common interests. My dream of uniting a more connected society has come true." - Yasmine El-Baggari, *Forbes* Magazine's "30 Under 30" issue, Founder of Voyaj.

Immediate Goals:

- Write your story: Take an hour (or two!) to sit down and write your story. Create a list of the challenges, setbacks, different pain points you encountered along the way. Write them down no matter how big or small. Honor your childhood and circumstances that have brought you to where you are. Find one individual to share your story with, allowing yourself to create a new awareness for how it has shaped you today.

<u>End-of-Chapter Exercise</u>

Describe a time when you were challenged with a particular fear. What did you do to overcome it? Who were you with? What did it take for you to confront it?

_____

_____

_____

_____

With the same fear you listed above, what is the absolute worst case scenario that would happen if that fear came true? Would that change you as a person? Would that reflect who you are?

_____

_____

_____

_____

Create your personal authentic story of your life up to this point in 6 words. You may use adjectives or nouns (Ex. Adventurous, motivating, full, resilient, courageous, unexpected, humble, uncertain,). Name two people that you will share this with this week.

_____

_____

_____

Recommended reading:

o *The Gifts of Imperfection: Let Go of Who You Think You're Supposed to be and Embrace Who You Are,* **by** Brené Brown
o *Start with Why: How Great Leaders Inspire Everyone to Take Action,* **by** Simon Sinek
o *The Big Leap: Conquer Your Hidden Fear and Take Life to the Next Level,* **by** Gay Hendricks
o *Callings: Finding and Following an Authentic Life,* **by** Gregg Levoy
o *The Exquisite Risk: Daring to Live an Authentic Life,* **by** Mark Nepo

CHAPTER FIVE

THE EMOTIONALGRIT KIT – USING EMPATHY TOOLS TO NAIL THE EMOTIONS GAME

"Life is too short for long-term grudges." – Elon Musk

Chapter Intention: I am prepared to live an exceptional life. Every day, I am building my emotional toolkit to allow me to draw wisdom, self-love, and experience. Each new morning allows me to practice and fulfill my promise to myself that I am growing and transforming in who I am meant to become.

Chapter Checklist

- Traditions are a part of the human experience. Are there any traditions you practice in your daily life?
- Do you celebrate the aspects of your uniqueness that light you up every single day? Making sure that your habits that you create in starting your day set you up to overflow onto those you serve. This sets the tone for your emotional mastery.
- Do you start your day in a rush, for the day to run you, or are you able to organize the day with proper reflection? In this chapter, we'll be tackling ways to slow your life down to include time tapping into your "happy place" to ensure your EmotionalGrit Kit is well equipped with essential tools for success.

As a woman and an entrepreneur, I often used to catch myself filling the cups of others before filling my own. From a cultural standpoint, this was expected. Happiness and fulfillment exists when you are in service to others. While theoretically this was true, if you are serving your families, communities, and teams from a half-filled cup then low-hanging emotions tend to rise to the surface. More specifically, resentment, anxiety, stress, and worry tend to arise if we are stretching ourselves too thin. You may think this is a selfish act. Yet, as in the airplane example of placing your oxygen mask on first before helping your friends and loved ones, the same principle applies here as well.

It wasn't until I started taking my future seriously (that is, diving into my own attitude and success) that I realized this important truth: Filling my cup needed priority. I had to operate out of a different mindset—a new way of thinking that helped me understand that I wasn't being selfish, but rather I was being responsible to my needs and my future. Putting others first had always been a trigger for me. For as long as I can remember, I've based my goals on other people's expectations, which profoundly affected my leadership, as well as the friendships and relationships that I attracted. It wasn't until I embraced the WHY that I could understand how this was holding me back.

The WHY includes:

- Understanding how my past experiences have shaped my outlook.
- Recognizing the importance of putting myself before others, so I can be a greater asset as a whole, fulfilled individual.
- Establishing a clear picture in my head that it was my obligation to make self-care a priority.
- Studying the characteristics of mentors, and global game changers: everyone from philosophers, to innovators, creators, and artists who made routines a must for their ability to thrive and affect the masses as a result.

The software tycoon and billionaire Sanjiv Sidhu says his methodology for sustaining willful and long-term tenacity is applying the 80/20 rule to how he governs his life as a father to his two daughters, a mentor to the many startups and entrepreneurs he advises, and CEO to the many projects and teams that he oversees. As he points out: "Don't let the small stuff get in the way."

In other words, 20% of what you do daily provides 80% of your happiness, your consistency, your mindset, and even your results.

Think about this for a moment: **Have you created a list of what truly makes you happy or keeps you at peace to begin the 24 hours that we all have every single day? If so what can you commit to daily that would give you 80% of your results?**

As a leader of your own life, the biggest factor affecting change is your ability to *choose* your emotional state. So if you are creating the tools in order to get you in that state, it will change the physiology of your body, and more specifically the biochemistry of your cells (which you will be guided through specifically throughout this chapter), but first: you have to understand that your attitude is everything.

The key driver for change will be your ability to show **enthusiasm**.

Ask yourself one important question: How often do you wake up with enthusiasm for the day ahead? It takes willpower and determination to commit to the results that we are seeking, what few are able to achieve.

> As a leader of your own life, the biggest factor affecting change is your ability to *choose* your emotional state.

Losing weight is a great example. You are aware of what needs to be done, yet the extra glass of wine, chocolate cake, or business meeting with the complimentary snack is sitting in front of you on the table—and it's hard to say no! It starts with creating and building the mental discipline, the awareness behind the decision making process. Why do you want to lose weight in the first place? To feel healthy, to look good, or both? What are some of the consequences if you eat that piece of chocolate, or indulge in an extra glass of wine? Will you be over your calorie limit for the day? It begins with these small questions to begin to peel back the layer and get to the root.

- Authenticity and self-mastery lead to your drive to self-care (fill your cup first before) you lead into the world.
- What are you willing to do and start your day with?

Traditional morning rituals around the world and why this is important

Ayurveda morning rituals to wake up to have been practiced for centuries in India and begin with getting up before sunrise and doing sun salutations offering gratitude to the sun for the day ahead.

- **First,** you take eleven deep inhale and exhale breaths from your belly to awaken your lungs and your internal system. This acts as a pumping mechanism awaking, cleansing, and detoxifying your system *before* you start your day.
- **Then**, you do a moving meditation form of qi-gong, awakening the chi within your body to invigorate the stagnant energy that has been dormant while you were sleeping. Specifically, our lymphatic system needs a shake up in the morning, and getting your blood circulation begins moving it through your cells, awakening your muscles, and releasing trapped energy in your lymphatic system for blood flow throughout the day.

Several religious practices have a special bell, tone, chant, or music as a way to set the tone and mood for the day ahead.

- Lighting incense or burning sage in the Hindu tradition has often been used as a morning practice to invoke and inspire clarity, calmness, creativity and readiness.
- Creating your personal "Morning Bliss" ensures that you are taking the time to full your cup so that you are fully loaded and operating from the Zen philosophy of "overflowing and outpouring onto others." It is the very core of empathetic leadership. Remember, to give empathy, we must offer it from a place of wholeness within ourselves. I have a strong belief that we are responsible for many things, but none more so than the attitude and energy we bring to each day.

The world needs your greatness!

Remember, leaders are not made overnight. There are certain processes and systems that some of the most thought-provoking influencers of our generation employ each day that make them successful, including having a routine the moment your feet hit the floor. Do you struggle to enter into your day with a clear vision, leaving yesterday's baggage behind? Many professionals state the best way to find purpose, is to *create* purpose. A morning routine will allow you to begin to navigate your day with meaningful activity. Whether journaling, sipping coffee on the porch, or mediating, a routine is a mandatory practice in making sure you are filling your cup first every single day so you can serve those around at your highest level.

Hear from some of today's leaders and how they start off their days

Former White House Fellow & Presidential fellow candidate, Dr. Reid Jilek who has served on several different boards ranging from biotechnology, engineering, and business doesn't classify himself as a morning person, yet his morning routine includes five key elements.

1. Movement
2. Spending time with wife
3. Reading something of interest
4. Classical Music
5. Breakfast

Now it doesn't have to be fancy, for you over-achievers out there! It can be small simple acts that you can enjoy every single morning no matter where you are, or how busy live gets. Think of this as your own personal time whether it is 5 minutes to 90 minutes as long as you can effectively be consistent. Scott Adams, creator of *Dilbert*, also starts each day with a routine. In fact, the first twenty minutes of Adams' day are the exact same every day. Starting with a protein bar and coffee, Adams states, "I give myself this "treat" knowing I can be trained like any other animal," he says. "And I want to train myself to enjoy waking up and being productive."

Just like the leaders above, you will want to explore whether a morning routine will help ignite purpose and passion into your day. (Hint: It will!) These morning processes will help fill your cup first so that at any given time when your emotional tank is getting low, you can draw from a reservoir of inner well-being to adjust your emotional state. Your emotional strength and how you respond to these situations helps you sail through sticky situations with grace and confidence, creating a ripple effect that can change your world.

Time to Check-in:

Please take five minutes and make a list of how you can begin your own "Morning Bliss". Name as many things as you possibly can that come to mind to create a perfect day for you.

For example: savoring your tea, journaling, listening to a podcast, playing with your children, working out, doing yoga, meditating, doing 50 pushups, dancing to your favorite song? You should have a list of at least five to ten things.

Creating your Morning Bliss routine

- From the list above, focus on three-to-five of those things you can consistently, and repeatedly do on a daily basis that would make you a better human for your family, spouse, and the people you serve.
- For example, it's non-negotiable for me: I must have my green juice and turmeric lemon water, meditate for five minutes, move my body for a minimum of ten minutes, journal, and read something inspiring anywhere in the world.
- What did you come up with?
- How much time does this require? Thirty-to-sixty minutes to fill your cup for the day.

- How early do you need to plan to get up in order to make sure this is part of your new human potential beginning tomorrow?

Fantastic! You now have your Morning Bliss routine. Beginning tomorrow, what 2 things will you incorporate to begin your self-care Morning Bliss?

Now Let's Begin Creating Your Emotionalgrit KIT!

This is essential for navigating your low-energy emotions, daily stress management kit, and the challenges that may arise during the seasons of life. These tools will help empower you and your teams to take accountability in times of adversity, yet more specifically provide you with easy solutions for your emotional endurance plan.

Here are four ways to use your EmotionalGRIT KIT to become a great leader:

1. Find Happy (no really!)

Finding a place of serenity will give you power over powerless situations. This could be something as simple as re-focusing your mind to a certain geographical place, or silently singing a song. When I am feeling that my mindset needs change, the first thing I do is play any 90's dance tune.

A leading professor of psychology, the late Christopher Peterson, was able to prove that becoming acutely aware of the life moments that give us greatest pleasure helps us maximize the amount of happiness we receive. He believes "happy places" should be three things: easy to remember, neutral and without penalty, always contributing to the meaning of our lives. Quite simply, one of the best ways to find a "happy place" is to use a positive memory. Try to find a memory that allows you to get completely lost in the smell, feeling and sight of what you once experienced. Once you find that memory, jot it down in a notebook. One thing I always do is encourage clients to keep a "Happy List" of places, memories, songs, and smells that have an instant and positive effect on their mood.

PLACE   MEMORY   SONG   SCENT

2. Jam It Out

Did you know that music has a dramatic effect on our mood? According to <u>Healthline</u>, research shows that listening to music can lift (or reinforce) your mood and ultimately lead to a greater quality of life.

Scientists at the University of Missouri have found that people can boost their mood simply by listening to upbeat music. Even better, *The Journal of Positive Psychology* found that people can successfully improve their moods and boost their overall happiness in just two weeks by incorporating music into their daily lives. Imagine the possibilities if you could incorporate music into your morning routine, or to help you find calm before bed. There are many ways to allow music into the moments of your life!

Dr. Frank Lipman, founder and director of Eleven-Eleven Wellness Center in New York City recommends musical time-outs. Dr. Lipman found that by taking time to listen and enjoy music, it calmed the body and brain, slowing the heart rate and helping to regulate breathing.

There are online sites such as Focus at will.com, Pandora, and Spotify on which you can choose binaural beats, which are brain radio wave frequencies that enhance certain neurological states to enhance your awareness, efficiency, deepen your relaxed state, revitalize, and even make you more focused at tasks.

- **Alpha** brain-waves: what we achieve when we are relaxed, or in a meditation non worry state.
- **Beta** brain waves: our waking consciousness and state of awareness/logical reasoning. We spend most of our day in this state, which can cause lots of toxic buildup—what author Brian Johnson calls, "gremlin poop". Deep sleep and meditation can help remove the buildup.
- **Delta** brain waves: this the deep sleep, or REM sleep state
- **Gamma**: your focused creativity brain wave.

Depending on the music genre, from classical to electronic, to ambient or even white noise, binaural beats mimic the relaxation state in your brain frequency to induce you into that state quicker and is a great hack for when you would like to catch up on sleep, or a quick nap to improve performance, productivity, and efficiency.

3. Allow yourself to be STILL

Meditation and guided visualization are both helpful exercises. But even more so, simply being still can have dramatic effects on the brain. Many of today's most impactful leaders find time to think, process, and reflect. In just five to ten minutes a day, you can create peaceful moments to inspire better decisions.

According to Dr. Frank Lipman, "When we are aware of our breathing, it helps to calm the body and mind. This calmness helps us be more aware of our thoughts and feelings and not being swept away with them." Breathing techniques do all the following to our body:

- Help release tension and energize us.
- Act as the perfect antidote to the fight-or-flight reaction.
- Detoxifies the buildup in our brains for consistently being in "beta mode" or "work mode" and has shown to increase levels of creativity from the pre-frontal cortex.
- Allow us be more present in every moment and lead to better focus and concentration on tasks and projects.
- Anchor us, and being more aware with our families, friends, and teams.

Can you breathe your way to good health? The International Foundation of Breathwork promotes and teaches various forms of yogic and breathing patterns for better oxygenation for physiologic health benefits. Dr. Andrew Weil Harvard trained professional offers this exercise to help you breathe more deeply, allowing your body to relax and recharge thus activating your parasympathetic system signaling the body for rest:

> Start by counting how many times you breathe each minute. In a relaxed sitting posture, most people breathe anywhere from 15 to 25 times a minute. (After practicing these exercises, your breathing rate may drop to as low as five times a minute, with a greatly increased level of oxygen use.)

> Lie down on either a bed or the floor. Place a fairly heavy book on your abdomen just below your navel.

> Breathe through your nose, inhaling in such a manner that you raise the book. When you exhale, the book should lower.

Continue practicing this until this breathing pattern becomes natural.

YOUR BRAIN WAVES

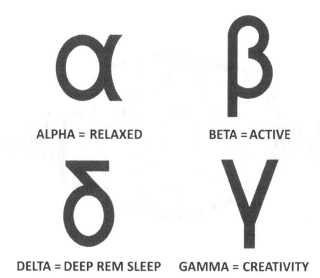

ALPHA = RELAXED   BETA = ACTIVE

DELTA = DEEP REM SLEEP   GAMMA = CREATIVITY

4. Consider Journaling

While it may seem like just another "to do," journaling has the power to dramatically enhance your day. Many CEOs and leaders I know begin each morning by journaling their intentions of the day and writing through difficult moments of confusion or change. Could there be actual health benefits to journaling? James Pennebaker, a psychologist at the University of Texas at Austin, believes that regular journaling strengthens immune cells, called T-lymphocytes. Dr. Pennebacker also believes that writing about stressful situations or moments of difficulty help individuals come to a deeper understanding of the grief process as a whole, allowing our brains and bodies to process change on a higher level, reducing the impact of stress on their life.

In fact, according to PsycCentral, journaling has the following benefits:

- **Clarifying your thoughts and feelings.** Do you ever seem all jumbled up inside, unsure of what you want or feel? Taking a few minutes to jot down your thoughts and emotions (no editing!) will quickly get you in touch with your internal world.
- **Knowing yourself better.** By writing routinely you will get to know what makes you feel happy and confident. You will also become clear about situations and people who are toxic for you, important information for your emotional well-being.
- **Reducing stress.** Writing about anger, sadness, and other painful emotions helps to release the intensity of these feelings. By doing so you will feel calmer and better able to stay in the present.
- **Solving problems more effectively.** Typically, we problem solve from a left-brained, analytical perspective. But sometimes the answer can only be found by engaging right-brained creativity and intuition. Writing unlocks these other capabilities, awakens different parts of the brain that we don't typically use and affords the opportunity for unexpected solutions to seemingly unsolvable problems.
- **Resolving disagreements with others.** Writing about misunderstandings rather than stewing over them will help you to understand another's point of view. And you just may come up with a sensible resolution to the conflict.

Midday Check-In:

Starting each day with a productive attitude is admirable, but do you often find that you struggle near the three p.m. mark? Here are some of my top productivity strategies that I've learned along the way. I've come across other "life hacks" that have helped me juggle all of the big projects in my life with much more ease, better efficiency, and in half the time.

1. Plan ahead and prioritize.

Accept you will not get it all done. Rather highlight the three big "bullets" or things you need/want to tackle on a certain day. For instance: I would save my planning for my next week on Sundays and devote an hour to what that next week looks like. Similarly, I plan out what times of the day are better for me to check my emails and respond to them (in one bunch). Get the idea?

2. Stick to time blocks

There are certain times in the day that you are more efficient. We all need breaks, and when you get into that sweet spot zone, it feels good! So perhaps, you want to get a workout in or need to conduct some meetings. Use the process of "chunking," so that your mind is focused on one task at hand, and therefore you are able to knock out what's needed for that task. For me, it's making sure most of my meetings and calls are done between one and six pm a few days a week. This allows me to deeply focus and be highly productive!

3. Focus and no turning back

Getting into the groove requires some aid; for me that's green tea and some binaural beats. For creativity to get my brain into the "gamma" state (the creativity state) I play some binaural beats and it makes a world of a difference.

4. Life: a sensory experience

Did you know that studies have shown that aromatherapy can significantly improve your productivity? University of Minnesota, Linda Halcon describes that essential oils and aromatherapy have benefits we haven't even begun to understand. Scents can literally awaken different aspects in our physiology making you more aware, change your brain chemicals for more focus, relaxation, productivity, and even curb hunger. Other changes can include activating the immune system, affecting blood pressure and stimulating digestion.

Here are 6 common scents used to elevate mood in various capacities that could add to your EmotionalGRIT.

1. **Lemon/Grapefruit:** This scent promotes concentration and has calming and clarifying properties that are helpful when you're feeling angry, anxious or run down. Lemon also has antiviral and antibacterial properties and can help fight sore throats and colds by boosting the body's immune system and improving circulation.

2. **Lavender:** This essential oil has calming properties that help control emotional stress. Lavender has a soothing effect on nerves and can relieve nervous tension and depression as well as treat headaches and migraines.

3. **Jasmine:** Like lavender, jasmine is also used to calm nerves, but this oil is also commonly used as an anti-depressant because of its uplifting capabilities that produce a feeling of confidence, optimism, and revitalized energy.

4. **Rosemary:** This is the perfect Monday morning pick-me-up. In addition to improving memory retention, rosemary has stimulating properties that fight physical exhaustion, headaches and mental fatigue. "It's excellent to use in the mornings when one needs a bit of help getting going," says Hawkins. Rosemary can also be used topically to relieve muscular aches and pains.

5. **Cinnamon:** The stimulating properties in cinnamon can help fight mental fatigue and improve concentration and focus.

6. **Peppermint:** Try peppermint when brainstorming. An energy booster, this scent invigorates the mind, promotes concentration and stimulates clear thinking.

Remember: For us to live our best life, I fully believe in the power of approaching each day intentionally and proactively designing how you fill your cup first so that you are best equipped to tackle the challenges that be arise. After all, you are now aware of your own set of tools for your emotional wellbeing. From repetitive activities or traditions, to morning routines and creating bliss, when we focus on lifting our mindsets to a place of meaningful productivity, we reach far greater inner strength resulting in outer success.

CREATING YOUR EMOTIONALGRIT KIT CHEAT-SHEET

MUSIC

• Upbeat playlist.
• Classical, binaural beasts, brainwave noise to elevate yourself and your efficiency.

NUTRITION

• Drink water!
• Consume superfoods like cinnamon, turmeric, chaga, spirulina, chia seeds, coconut oil, flaxseeds, ashwaganda, astragaulus, cocoa, etc.

SCENTS

Incense, candles, essential oils (breathe some of your favorite scents).

MOVEMENT

• Emotion-> energy in motion.
• Move your body! Set a timer every hour to do 10 jumping jacks, 10 high kicks, 10 squats, and 10 pushups.

BREATHWORK

Deep breathing 3x in your belly to activate your parasympathetic system .

POSITIVE BOOKS /IAM STATEMENTS/QUOTES

List some of your favorites. Where can you post them? Desktop, phone, create a document for easy reach?

PODCASTS/MOVIES /FUNNY CLIPS

Humor, entertaining, enlightening, these can shift your mood in an instant.

MINDFULNESS /MEDITATION

All you need to start with is 2-3 mins. Silence. Easy breathing.

HUMAN INTERACTION

Who lights you up, who can you think about that puts a smile on your face? Who can you spend some time with or call? List them!

GRIT perspectives on drive and enthusiasm

"It all started with a bus stop. I was a statistic. A young African-American man who was homeless, jobless and a high school dropout. Call it a God wink or 'aha' moment, but I decided to change that day. The journey has been long, but I not only broke free from poverty and the lower rungs of conscious sabotage, but transcended it completely. Both dark and light are teachers. And without darkness there can be no light. So the past, the struggles, the obstacles all have been necessary components of my climb to the top and to this day serve me. When I think of Grit, I think of the caterpillar and this concept of imaginal cells. Essentially imaginal cells lay dormant until the last part of the caterpillar dies. Then all of the sudden these imaginal cells kick on and the caterpillar self-actualizes, becoming its highest self—a butterfly. My favorite line comes from a dialogue in Rocky III, where he is speaking to his son. 'It's not about getting hit. It's how many times you can get hit, and get back up again.' Getting back off that mat has been really hard some days, but if I didn't have drive, I probably would have just continued to lay there; that's GRIT." – Brandon Collinsworth, CEO Real Results

"Becoming an entrepreneur in 2009 to start my own production company and then my own women's networking initiative is probably the hardest thing I have ever done. Hard because, as the saying goes, it takes about 4-5 years before one understands how to make money and be solvent. But each day leading up to the fourth year, has been laced with second guessing, feelings of failure, and questioning what I'm doing. When a woman walks up to me and tells me she **got a job because of my introductions or events, it easily erases all that."** – Joya Dass, Bloomberg Financial/CSNBC Newsanchor, Documentary Filmmaker, CEO LadyDrinks Global

Immediate Goal:

30 day Challenge: Practice your Morning Bliss routine that you created from this chapter for the next 30 days. Start with 2-3 of the things which you can pick that are small, and simple from the EmotionalGRIT kit in the back resources of the book.

End-of-Chapter Exercise

Name three things that *drive* your habits, patterns, and current decision-making? (For example, what has been your motivation, your purpose, your why for the things that you do? Is it family, money, making your parents proud, solving a global problem?)

_____

_____

_____

With the GRIT characteristic of enthusiasm (more specifically your attitude), how do you currently use this in your daily life? What triggers the opposite? What things can you do to be in charge of the attitude you bring into each situation?

_____

_____

_____

Beginning with ten minutes each day, how will you choose to elevate your mood? Write your top three responses below.

_____

_____

_____

Recommended reading:

- *What the Most Successful People Do Before Breakfast,* by Laura Vanderkam
- *The Power of Habit: Why We Do What We Do in Life and Business,* by Charles Duhigg
- *Making Habits, Breaking Habits: Why We Do Things, Why We Don't, and How to Make Any Change Stick,* by Jeremy Dean
- *Nudge: Improving Decisions About Health, Wealth, and Happiness,* by Richard H. Thaler and Cass R. Sunstein
- *Switch: How to Change Things When Change Is Hard,* by Chip Heath and Dan Heath

PART 3

GROW. **REVEAL.**
INNOVATE. TRANSFORM.

Reveal
To *Accept the Past is to Move Forward*

"Only by owning our unique story, can we reveal its hidden gifts to the world."

Ever since childhood, Peter Diamandis was fascinated with space travel.

His parents were Greek immigrants in Bronx, New York. Against all odds, a young Peter embraced his love of space. He owned this far-out passion, winning the Estes Rocket Design competition at age 12. Diamandis likened his desire for space travel to his father's desire to migrate from Greece to America. He championed his father's bold exploration and to him, a generation on, his quest for going into space is the same as what his father did. Over the years of his life, this obsession with space has revealed many beautiful gifts to the world. By remaining authentic to his passions and purpose, futurist Peter Diamandis has sat on the boards of and founded many a groundbreaking project, most notably Singularity University in Silicon Valley, which was created to develop and harness exponential technologies to solve large global challenges. He also created the Xprize, which used the spirit of competition to recruit talented teams around the world to develop a vehicle capable of low-orbit, commercial space travel. The prize was ten million dollars and was won in 2004, proving that a private group of committed people could do what NASA hadn't managed in decades.

In Peter's words, "You get what you incentivize." Peter's high level of EmotionalGRIT and visionary ability to build the impossible has revealed breakthroughs that are changing the landscape of the evolving world.

What unique gifts do you have to reveal to the world? You have an entire lifetime. Begin now.

CHAPTER SIX

HAVING COURAGE
TO FEEL FEAR

"People grow through experience if they meet life honestly and courageously. This is how character is built." – Eleanor Roosevelt

Chapter Intention: I hold myself responsible to approach each relationship, situation, and my own emotions with courage and forgiveness. I recognize my need to articulate my story in a way that helps me learn from my past, but not be chained to it.

Chapter Checklist

- Have you ever kept a mental list of people who have done you wrong? Holding in anger, resentment, and negativity has a dramatic effect on your health and outlook.
- Do you celebrate even your smallest moments of courage, like walking up the stairs instead of taking the elevator, having a difficult conversation, saying 'no' to make time for other priorities, or choosing to eat healthier when fast food sounds just so much better?
- What is holding you back? Can you identify three situations or experiences that are keeping you harnessed to baggage from the past?

The Source of Courage

There have been fascinating studies digging deep into where courage comes from. Two curious Israeli scientists recently discovered one possible source of our courage—and it involved MRI machines and snakes. Yadin Dudai and Uri Nili from the Weizmann Institute of Science in Rehovot, Israel decided to use MRI technology to watch how the human brain responded when presented with images of something most people fear: snakes. *Scientific American* explains:

> "*Fear of the snake manifests itself in two ways – either you simply say, "I'm afraid," or your body says it for you, with sweat. The mechanics of courage in the brain, it seems, involves a competition. When fear reaches a certain threshold, pushing both your subjective*

feeling of it and your bodily sweat, you would succumb. Your amygdala drives that fear, but internal disagreement overcomes it. The agent behind this disagreement is the sgACC. It acts to control and suppress bodily fear responses, and sends nerve projections into the amygdala that shut it down."

For the first time, researchers were able to see an act of fear and courage played out for the human eye to see. This allowed Dudai and Nili to dig deeper into what often controls human emotion: an all-important choice between flight and fight.

I believe we have a sort of internal MRI, if you will; one that is one-third each hindsight, audacity, and emotional memory. Our internal MRI scans our feelings about our experiences each and every day—and our feelings, or the moods that develop from those feelings—as a check to tell us if something is truly bothering our psyche.

Let's pretend for one moment that you are part of a study about fear and courage like the one described above. You lay down quietly, wondering what pictures you'll be shown in the MRI. But instead of viewing snakes, you are shown highlights of moments of shame or guilt from your life as the MRI scans your brain. As you react to the imagery, you're given the option of ending the study (fleeing in fear) or sticking it out (choosing courage.) In our everyday lives, you are given the choice to allow our internal MRI's to scan memories, giving us the chance to make important decisions. What will you choose to do?

A list no one thinks they want

Have you ever thought where some of your fears stem from? Have you examined how your culture and life experience shape your identities? Or how they cause you to make the same deep decisions over and over and over again? Actually, there are patterns that cause you to carry on the fears and anxieties of the past. Failure and not achieving my vision of perfection debilitated me in being able to be authentic with how I was living my life. It was deeply rooted in the cultural obligations and expectations in family pride, legacy and preservation of my Filipino-Indian heritage. It was also based on the attachments I had to these thought patterns in my head which affected my fear pattern.

When we choose to be ruled by fear, and specifically when we allow the not-yet-happened to subsume our personal power, we've given up the only freedom we have: the freedom to choose.

It takes tremendous courage to chart a different direction. Fear limits us to thinking within a certain box. Learning to look past memories, pain, and experiences that may have initially wounded us in some capacity also may lead to triumphant blessings. In order to have the full understanding and awareness of these internal triggers that show up in your work and business life, you must allow your brain the ability to process the *why*. In order to begin to work past fears and forgive our past stories, we must first lay down the foundation around the culture of fear.

Yale Center of Emotional Intelligence psychologist Daniel Cordero talks about different root cultures of fear that shape our current society and how it governs our decision-making process as a result.

CULTURES OF FEAR

3 FEAR CULTURES

1 **CULTURE OF AVERSION**
"This isn't enough" so you do whatever it takes to avoid shame.

2 **CULTURE OF SCARCITY**
"There isn't enough" so you become hypercompetitive, over protective/selfish.

3 **UNWORTHINESS**
"I'm not enough" so self-acceptance becomes conditional; failure will happen, since expectations can never be met.

Cultures fall into these categories:

- familial
- organizational
- global
- national
- communal

How they affect and make up your mode of thinking is expressed in the following ways:

- behaviors
- beliefs
- values
- symbols
- relationships

These can all comprise your internal belief systems that you have built up around a subject. For instance, the cultural belief I had growing up that was ingrained in my head was that I could not bring home anything less than an A grade to my parents, and I couldn't date anyone who was African American or Muslim.

Now, diving deeper into this conversation there are three main ways this affects us in our daily decision making and can be a big game changer in revealing and understanding a different perspective that can have significant effects from today onward.

1. **Culture of Aversion**: "this isn't enough," so you do whatever it takes to avoid shame.
2. **Culture of Scarcity**: "there isn't enough," so you become hypercompetitive, over protective/selfish.
3. **Unworthiness**: "I'm not enough," so self-acceptance becomes conditional; failure will happen, since expectations can never be met.

For example, if you have grown up with an overachieving mindset, along with your attachment to success it is vital to you experiencing shame for the family name, parents, society you may make decisions in your life that no matter the amount of monetary success, accolades, and awards, it will never be enough.

Or if you think that the market is saturated with too many businesses similar to yours, you may base your decision making on jealousy, greed, and fear that there isn't enough for everyone, therefore I have to protect my assets, hide my business plan, and make sure no one knows my secrets to success.

In the culture of unworthiness, if you are attached to the notion of always having to prove to the world that you are worthy, and you don't celebrate your wins or appreciate the small milestones that you have crossed, nothing will ever be good enough. You will consistently be judging, overanalyzing, perfecting, and procrastinating based on this fear.

This is how unhealthy communication and conflict can arise in your life based on some of these inherent governing systems. If one of your triggers has been to win the approval of your strict father, you will do whatever it takes to gain the approval or validation from your boss, friends, or significant other. On the contrary, if you were told that you were an awful (fill in the blank) you may work extra hard to overcompensate and make sure you are not living in fear of that shameful comment.

The fact is, your brain does every day. From muscle memory to mental memories, we use knowledge of the past to make decisions on the future. This is one reason that allowing your brain to complete the positive cycle of thought and feeling is so vital to your future as a leader and a rounded human being.

> From muscle memory to mental memories, we use knowledge of the past to make decisions on the future.

Now that you have a better understanding of your patterns of your decision-making, you can be fully conscious and question yourself as to why is this coming up. **Do I really believe this, or is that something that is part of my programming?** You can begin to cultivate the empathy of those around you and their perspective and lens as they make decisions.

This is vital for any relationship, and can prove to be powerful in scaling and growing your team, as well as having a thriving family and social life—just by being more cognizant of other people's cultures of fear.

> ## <u>Check-in Exercise</u>
>
> - Which of the three cultures of fear have shaped your life thus far?
> - Can you think of one particular instance where your behavior pattern has caused you to either hire the wrong person, choose a bad business decision, or continue to stay in the same situation?
>
> In each of the three cultures of fear, choose one and allow yourself to experience the discomfort and sensation of the unknowing. (This is when we grow and expand the most.)

<u>Courage to Forgive and Release</u>

As humans, we have done everything in our power to distract ourselves from feeling our emotional triggers. It's in our DNA to avoid pain. So we do the things as humans to deflect the pain. We are taught that to "feel emotions" is a sign of weakness and lack of strength, so we pacify them with the external desires for food, sex, alcohol, drugs, busyness, and even problems. Yes, problems. You ask someone how their day is, and it becomes competition of whose problem is worse: growing up, my aunts were notorious for this. One would complain she had a headache, and the other would fire back that she had a headache and pains in her leg that lasted for days. It's our human involuntary response to hold on to problems because they also give us something to complain about and therefore distract ourselves from our deepest, darkest fears.

> We are taught that to "feel emotions" is a sign of weakness and lack of strength, so we pacify them with the external desires for food, sex, alcohol, drugs, busyness, and even problems.

As people looking to uplevel your potential, take a look at this list of the common distracting responses that many leaders I've come across in 45 countries have related to and has become a highly useful tool and assessment in assessing CEOs and leaders that I often work with:

- Imposter syndrome
- Consistently pressured to thrive and provide results
- Feel alone/lonely that you are the only one capable of execution
- Lack of trust in your teammates/colleagues/employees
- Work/life balance (home life is under stress)/ relationship stress
- Shame/vulnerability as a sign of weakness
- Internalizing stress, and feel like you cannot ask for help
- Feel like you need to wear a "mask"
- Fear of failure
- Fear of the grandeur of success
- Fear of never being enough
- Fear of being incompetent
- Fear of judgment
- Fear of rejection
- Expectation of perfection in your execution of ideas, projects, and even life
- Feel you cannot stop or take a break
- Fear of not enough time, not enough resources
- Intense anxiety/lack of sleep/imbalanced stress

> It takes courage to break outside of the box
> and live beyond the stories of your past.

Yet now you are fully gaining the tools and insights to think differently. You are already 70% ahead of others because you are spending the time, making the commitment, and driven to revolutionize your thinking. Some of the greatest philosophers of our time discuss how forgiveness is a powerful vehicle allowing you to move on, that it isn't about the other person. Yet, it allows you the space and freedom to reveal a better version of yourself. Allowing the gentle self-acceptance that comes with being human and making better decisions from the previous experience is the key here.

> Life lessons will keep showing up in your
> life—until you decide to choose differently.

We can choose courage even in the smallest of ways, by writing down three things that scare us every day and how we will take one single step that day to unmask or deconstruct the fear. Even the tiniest step can have a measurable impact on your mood and your outcomes!

One of the first lists I encourage you to write is a list of people that you need to give yourself the courage to forgive and let go.

Forgiveness is one of the most difficult steps you can take—and it is steeped in courageous action. To forgive is to essentially say out loud: I am letting go of any emotion regarding this person, this experience, this failure, this set-up, and the actions others chose. Highlighting an often under-looked quality that all empathetic leaders need, the perceived loss of power that forgiveness brings is the opposite of what the situation gives us: it gives us our power back.

In her scientific study of forgiveness, Katheryn Rhoads Meek suggests that forgiveness brings powerful therapeutic benefits that create wholeness within our mind and body- albeit deeply-rooted in religion, but having far-reaching context, in a secular world.

> *"The Campaign for Forgiveness Research cites recent studies showing that the practice of forgiveness is directly related to emotional healing and the building of peaceful communities. The practical and therapeutic effects of forgiveness are far 90 Forgiveness ranging, and can be seen in various personal and social contexts: among Vietnam veterans coping with post-traumatic stress disorders; among victims of sexual abuse and domestic violence; among HIV/AIDS patients; and among the diverse clusters of people facing end-of-life issues. Given the link between health and forgiveness, is it any wonder that many people now think forgiveness can reduce the severity of heart disease, prolong the life of cancer patients, and reduce levels of crime (by quenching the desire for revenge)?"*

> # Forgiveness is one of the most difficult steps you can take—and it is steeped in courageous action.

Katheryn pointedly showcases that forgiveness creates hope within individuals and communities as a whole. Her research joins the Mayo Clinic and other reputable institutions in citing the health benefits of forgiveness. The Mayo Clinic states that forgiveness can lead to healthier relationships, greater wellbeing, less anxiety, stress and hostility and lower blood pressure, among other important items, including improved heart health and higher self-esteem.

The myth of security

Throughout the course of life as we identified in the earlier chapters, the idea of fulfilling our basic needs as humans is dependent upon feeling safe, secure, or comforted under Maslow's hierarchy. This idea of 'security' promotes deep levels of attachment where it can prevent you from leaping into the unknown of 'uncertainty' which can contribute to profound levels of growth, rooted in courage. So many of us are more likely to simply reside in our 'safe' circumstances because it is often easy, predictable, and safe rather than facing some of our own fears head on and rising to the bravado of uncertainty with the potential to soar.

Seeking perfection is really an intense fear of failure

In Girls Who Code founder Reshma Saujani's TED talk, she discusses the importance of teaching young women that bravery creates a much more resilient self, while perfection tears down the psyche. Reshma so accurately pointed out that we were training our children in two different ways: keeping their gender in mind even if we didn't mean to. She states:

> *"Most girls are taught to avoid failure and risk. To smile pretty, play it safe, get all A's. Boys, on the other hand, are taught to play rough, swing high, crawl to the top of the monkey bars and then jump off head first. By the time they're adults and whether they're negotiating a raise or even asking someone out on a date, men are habituated to take risk after risk. They're rewarded for it. It's often said in Silicon Valley that no one even takes you seriously unless you've had two failed startups. In other words, we're raising our girls to be perfect and we're raising our boys to be brave."*

Especially for female leaders, GRIT is mischaracterized as "stick-to-it-ness." The problem we now know is that pivoting and working SMARTER (not harder!) is what will help you reach the next summit of your career. A recent report by Harvard Business Review found that men will apply for a job if they feel they meet 60% of the qualifications, while women only apply if they feel the position is a perfect fit. The study mentioned:

> *"According to the self-report of the respondents, the barrier to applying was not lack of confidence. In fact, for both men and women, "I didn't think I could do the job well" was the least common of all the responses. Only about 10% of women and 12% of men indicated that this was their top reason for not applying... In other words, people who weren't applying believed they needed the qualifications not to do the job well, but to be hired in the first place. They didn't see the hiring process as one where advocacy, relationships, or a creative approach to framing one's expertise could overcome not having the skills and experiences outlined in the job qualifications."*

To be brave, we must take great risks that often seem unimaginable at first thought. Keeping Reshma Saujani in mind, have you taken a "safe" road that's led to you wondering how you'd live a passionate and well-rounded life? Reshma ran for Congress (and failed) at 33 years old. What's the last great risk you've taken?

Check-in Exercise

How to deal with imposter syndrome? When the negative self-talk arises practice the following:

1. Awareness: Understand and pay attention to the negative talk. "I am not good enough, I don't have the right team, I don't have the skill set" etc.
2. Depersonalize and Accept: Look at it from the third person. For example, instead of "I'm not good enough for the position" say I notice that this thought of feeling not good enough is coming up.
3. Look at it as if you are reading it on a billboard.
4. Realize it is a thought you are experiencing and the "why behind it". For example, when you "label it" you can look at it as an outsider and acknowledge it. Is it fear of rejection, shame? etc.
5. Write it down.
6. Congrats, you have just conquered the art of turning around a negative thought.

BRAVE = TAKE RISKS THAT ARE UNIMAGINABLE

Take a moment. Your bag is spilling open

In meeting new leaders and CEOs, I often witness a lack of forgiveness and the internal shame, baggage, and resentment it brings both in the boardroom and at home. One of the most important steps I take with individuals in leading them through the GRIT process is helping clients to understand the burden and weight of decisions. I think of carrying emotion and a refusal to forgive almost like sprinting through the airport with a ripped and heavy paper bag. Every 100 feet or so, we must shift the bag in our arms and try in a new way to contain what is in our bag—but without fail, it keeps ripping and things spill out. Courageously choosing forgiveness is like taking time at the check-in desk to re-pack items before running down the concourse. While forgiveness clearly takes more than a few minutes, in the greater timeline of our life, choosing forgiveness is the difference of a hurried, ripped bag and a slower, more pleasant walk. Life is an experience that's meant to be treasured, reflected upon and celebrated.

> Carrying more than you're built to handle will diminish the chances of living in the present.

While you might understand the "why" of forgiveness, have you actually practiced the act? Remember my belief that each day, we can move the needle on three items we fear? Choosing courage is the exact same as choosing forgiveness. Practice in small ways: smile at the distracted driver that cuts you off, wave at the child making a face while you're waiting in line, and most important, practice kindness and a gentler spirit and allow yourself to feel more support from its biggest critic: you!

One of my favorite quotes is from Nelson Mandela:

> "I learned that courage was not the absence of fear, but the triumph over it. The brave man is not he who does not feel afraid, but he who conquers that fear."

You're prepared to take on the task of not only choosing courage but also starting to let go *and* forgive those that have hurt you. This is a BIG step in the GRIT process!

GRIT perspectives on forgiveness and resilience

"My life has been one, bit GRIT. I encountered severe (sexual, verbal and non-verbal) abuse from when I was a baby until adulthood. I thought of myself as a victim, until I discovered that everything I attracted was inside of me. As a result, I was severely overweight most of my life, and at my heaviest I weighed 302 pounds and I am 5'8. Being adopted as an Indonesian young girl into a European family I was always different, I stood out and I so badly wanted to fit in. It had me even getting involved with a love relationship that had me being illegally sex-trafficked for 8 months. Feeling trapped, betrayed, and a victim, the only way I could heal this cycle of my life was to love myself first. From a place of self-compassion, and an understanding of all my decisions up until that point of my life, forgiveness for me to start new was vital. It was pivotal to my growth in all aspects. Through loving myself I could finally forgive myself and the perpetrators. It has allowed me to over the last three years be in the best shape of my life, now training to be a fitness competitor, beginning several wellness businesses across the Netherlands, and to cultivate the most loving and extraordinary life partner." – Naomi L., Fitness Expert, PR executive, Utrecht, Netherlands

"In dealing with a variety of challenges I've found it to be very important to have a strong internal compass that allows one to move forward with the head held high irrespective of the circumstances. Entrepreneurship tests this characteristic continuously. Working from government and politics on President Obama's campaign, to the media, and even in social enterprises in rebuilding a new Haiti with sustainability if have been exposed to the challenges of forgiveness. It is often seen as freeing someone else

> *from guilt, but I see it from two perspectives. First, it not only liberates others from errors they may have committed, but also one's self from carrying unnecessary burdens. Second, I fundamentally believe that every person always does their best and at our core we are one. Accordingly, in forgiveness we show humility, understanding while ultimately forgiving ourselves."* — Jacques Philippe Piverger, Investor, Serial Entrepreneur, Young Global Leader, World Economic Forum

Immediate Goal:

Which of the fears listed have you identified and what is one way that you will be more mindful in the "REVEAL" process of GRIT in your own life?

End-of-Chapter Exercise

Often we look to external situations and sources of our pain when we practice forgiveness. Is there something you have been waiting to forgive, or let go of that sits within YOU? Perhaps it's a past situation, something that still triggers you, caused a big challenge. Write it down.

_____

_____

_____

_____

Do you acknowledge and celebrate even your smallest moments of victory? While we live in a culture of "accolade trophies" we often neglect to acknowledge our moments courageous moments. What's one thing you've done lately to celebrate? (Go for a walk out in nature, spend time at a spa, treat yourself to a movie etc).

_____

_____

_____

_____

We struggle every day to accept things we cannot control. Instead of abiding by a mantra someone else has written, can you write your own "serenity" statement? Here's mine:

Today, I have the courage to accept what lies ahead of me, the resilience to complete any difficult task and the ability to let people, situations and feelings go if they are holding me back.

Write yours below.

_____

_____

_____

_____

Recommended reading:

o *Forgive and Forget: Healing the Hurt We Didn't Deserve,* by Lewis B. Smedes

o *The Pursuit of Perfect: How to Stop Being a Perfectionist,* by Tal Ben Shahar

o *How to Be an Imperfectionist: The New Way to Self-Acceptance, Fearless Living, and Freedom from Perfectionism,* by Stephen Guise

CHAPTER SEVEN

YOUR BOUNDARIES VS. BOUNDLESS CURIOSITY

"The important thing is not to stop questioning.
Curiosity has its own reason for existing." – Albert Einstein

Chapter Intention: I prepare myself daily by whispering to myself the importance of establishing and keeping healthy boundaries for work, home and all relationships in-between. My boundaries do not define me, but they offer a reminder that my life is my own. I have no one to answer to but myself.

Chapter Checklist

- As human beings, we are connected by a myriad of behaviors, none more so than the inability to let ourselves be creative and ask "why?" To become the best leader we can be, we must always ask "but then what?" after each solution.
- Boundaries are often undefined for many reasons, but often by guilt. When we carry guilt with us into our daily life, we are often unable to build (and keep!) healthy boundaries that would make our lives easier—emotionally, physically, spiritually and otherwise.
- There's a sort of dualism in many boardrooms and bedrooms. We all struggle to walk the fine line of wanting to both experience more (being curious) and delivering more (overachieving.)

The Source of Curiosity

Through the **Reveal** process of EmotionalGRIT, you have already begun to release items from your past, acknowledging their presence, understanding their importance, and becoming more accepting of yourself and those around you.

Cultivating the new landscape of your human potential, operating from a lens of curiosity to wonder, to discover and to ask questions is so important for growth in yourself, your business, your influence, and most of all, the impact that you can have on society. My fascination with human dynamics and with fully understanding the reasons behind our decision-making starts with having the desire to want to learn more.

Tony Robbins, the international personal development guru with 30 plus years of teaching, coaching and consulting for over 22 businesses combined worth over a billion in assets, describes the six main desires of every person:

1. **Certainty**: need sense of safety, security, consistency, comfort.
2. **Variety**: fun, spontaneity, surprise, discovery, new hobby
3. **Connection/love**: relationships, serving people, family,
4. **Significance**: importance, distinction, recognition, ego, differentiation
5. **Growth**: learning new things, expanding business, intellect
6. **Contribution**: leaving a legacy, creating impact, donating/serving your gifts

A MODERN TAKE ON MASLOW & HUMAN NEEDS

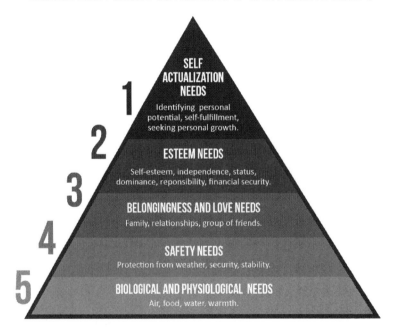

Robbins calls these the "Six Human Needs" and advises analyzing them to create a path to fulfillment. We're going to use them as a basis for another concept, one that we believe sparks adventure, fulfillment, and creative leadership: the magic of curiosity.

> My fascination with human dynamics and with fully understanding the reasons behind our decision-making starts with having the desire to want to learn more.

Spend some time thinking what *your* top two values are; in other words, what drives your motivation? What about those around you? This is one of the prime examples of how you can cultivate a sense of curiosity in your outlook and in architecting new leadership. I've had companies that utilize different methods of behavior analyses to build exponentially impactful teams. But what about doing this with your family, friends, and children? Do this for the ones that you love, in order to create stronger, deeper bonds, and recognize the differences—and perhaps shift to a new value.

For a long time, based on my cultural views of fear, my two main desires were always significance and variety. I needed to feel important based on my upbringing, and my love of travel and different business projects fueled an insatiable thirst for more.

The majority of the clients and overachievers that I've come across struggle with certainty and significance. Certainty or "safety" means you need to be in control, that things have to be predictable, and that there needs to be a certain amount of comfort in knowing the outcome. The notion of significance means consistently striving and desiring to be important—within your work, yourself, and amongst your community.

While none of these are bad values, the way that you approach your values will evolve, and to have a better grasp of how your current values have guided your life (the good, the bad, and the ugly) will help provide a better framework for choosing differently. As you become more aware and accept (be honest!), it will make the Reveal and Innovate process on your Emotional GRIT journey much smoother.

So, now it's your turn.

Take a moment to reflect and think about how you have been governing your life up until this point.

Which two values did you have at the top of your list?

What about you? Jot the first two that resonate with you, and beside it write some of the reasons how it has affected your decision making.

_____

_____

_____

_____

Keeping those values in the back of your mind, begin to curiously discover what values of which you desire more.

Every tiny, beautiful child is born with the innate ability to be curious. At a young age, children learn that curiosity is both important and dangerous. Children also learn the importance of safety and protection, but are often guided into believing that their role in life is to pacify and create happiness in others; this causes a deterioration of boundaries. First, we'll tackle the importance of curiosity, then we'll look at how curiosity and boundaries can work together to create a meaningful, introspective, and successful life.

Why curiosity?

In a roundabout way, we can link curiosity to success at multiple levels. Curiosity helps with learning, focus, brain production, and even mood; it allows for expansion in thinking, problem solving, and solution seeking. My father always said, "Don't come to me with a problem unless you have a solution."

The biggest innovators of our time were not afraid to leap outside the confines of mediocrity and were boundless in their vision because of their quest and pursuit for a better way. Is that what determines our evolution as humans? Simply because when we are more aware, we know better? When we know better, we have a greater understanding of the challenges, risks, and obligations that are in front of us, therefore choosing more wisely as a result. As we make better and more conscious decisions, we can practice more empathy as a result, and can then put forth grand ideas that can collectively contribute to solving bigger challenges in our communities and networks as a result.

> The biggest innovators of our time were not afraid to leap outside the confines of mediocrity and were boundless on their vision because of their quest and pursuit for a better way.

So how can you become a better question-asker? It definitely begins with ruling out judgment or pre-determined answers. Not thinking that because you know the same employee for the past 20 years that you know all that they are feeling. Or anticipating the reactions of your spouse in not tending to simple commitments. Ask questions that can lead you to a different discussion—exploring the art of inquisition. Discovering that maybe the person that you know so well may have a different perspective on the subject. This requires patience and commitment to knowing this is exactly why EmotionalGRIT is a journey.

What about our brain?

The part of our brain that controls our creativity and higher thinking process, referred to as the "third eye" for the ancient Buddhist/Hindu traditions, is neuroscientifically-speaking the medial pre-frontal cortex of the brain, which on PET scans is shown to be the most active immediately after meditation. This is also part of the brain that is activated during calm states, i.e. when there is no fear or danger of threat present. (The opposite of the cortisol-inducing response to the brain.)

Therefore, it allows for higher levels of thinking, awareness, presence, and catapulting your human potential. Neuroscientist and professor Charan Ranganath of the University of California focused his study on the analysis of curiosity activation and its effects in overall expansive thinking. He discovered that curiosity not only prepares the brain for higher levels of creativity, but increased rates of long-term memory as well. A more curious subject was prepared for more sensory input and experienced increased dopamine output (the brain chemical that controls pleasure). The study focused on what happens to a brain when it's focusing on learning or being creative, and as with the Israeli study on our reaction to scary images, this one also used an MRI—minus the snakes!)

Participants were asked to memorize trivia and the results were, yes, curious:

"When the participants' curiosity was piqued, the parts of their brains that regulate pleasure and reward lit up. Curious minds also showed increased activity in the hippocampus, which is involved in the creation of memories. "There's this basic circuit in the brain that energizes people to go out and get

things that are intrinsically rewarding, this circuit lights up when we get money, or candy. It also lights up when we're curious. Indeed, when the researchers later tested participants on what they learned, those who were more curious were more likely to remember the right answers." – NPR.org

When we learn something with true curiosity, (that is, *we want to learn*) we're more likely to retain the information. Dopamine is a neurotransmitter that our brain produces to entice us into completing actions and is mainly responsible for discovery and curiosity. This is generally called the 'get it done' hormone allowing for concentration, drive, happiness, and as a result we tend to focus better and are able to have more long-term success.

Brain Food?

When Dopamine wears off, it produces another hormone prolactin which has the complete opposite, which causes low energy, irritability, and even depression. Which is the reason why it can become addicting in reaching that euphoric state.

Six ways to enhance Dopamine naturally:

- Body movement
- Comfort food cravings
- Laughter
- Music
- Take up a new project, or adventure
- Sensory stimulation-scents or different smells, touching or feeling

Seratonin is the neurotransmitter mainly produced in our digestive tract fully responsible for our mood, brain signals for appetite, sexual function, and sleep patterns.

Oxytocin, another vital hormone that is directly responsible for elevating mood. It is also known as the 'cuddle or the bonding hormone' which provides the sweet sauce for human connection that can be attained through social bonding, touch, and long term relationships.

Collectively all of these essential brain nutrients when functioning properly and understanding their roles within your body, you can become more aware of the imbalances that can occur because of a variety of reasons. Gaining the knowledge here will keep you better equipped of why your energy can drop, how important it is to keep your nutrition in alignment, to be in your best brain state, and how to enhance your brain power and productivity especially during stressful times. Also, you are more aware of what happens when you are lacking and when your body craves certain foods, or when you are fatigued, not sleeping, or in a slump. You are in the driver's seat. You are in control. You are building your EmotionalGRIT kit as the pieces are slowly coming together.

DOPAMINE DEFICIT

PARKINSON-LIKE SYMPTIONS
• Slow reaction time
• Anergia"

DEPRESSION & CRAVING

OCD-LIKE SYMPTIONS
• Obsessive thoughts
• Compulsive behaviours

ANHEDONIA
• "Pleasure Center" dysfunction

IMPULSIVITY
• Suicide/aggression
• Susceptibility to "cue triggers"

SERATONIN DEFICIT

<u>**Emotion = Energy in Motion**</u>

The goal is to circulate the lymph system—to move the stagnant stale energy created by sitting on our sofas, at our computer desks, and in our cars, all for hours on end—and rejuvenate ourselves, shaking up our physiological level to be our highest emotional and energetic state.

Move!

One of the best ways to increase dopamine is to *move* your body every single day. Consider adding exercise to your morning routine, as we discussed earlier in the book. Dancing, pushups, plank, jumping jacks, running in place, and stretching. A simple hack for you busy overdoers: set an alarm on your phone at the top of each hour to move! More important, exercise moves the stale energy and "stuff" in your lymphatic system so that you have a better mental state. Additionally, this not only keeps your body in great shape, but it clears the mind and allows your body to better process thoughts, feelings and issues of stress and anxiety.

Meditate

Hopefully you are practicing some of the meditation and breathing techniques outlined earlier in the book. Besides bringing your mind and soul to a centered state, meditation can increase dopamine levels, allowing you to better focus and push-through difficult situations and projects with greater ease. If meditation isn't your style, consider spending time in quiet reflection or prayer. Prayer, mindful reflection, and meditation all have the same benefit: larger amounts of brain power.

Music, Music, Music

From ancient chanting beats, to optimizing your brain function with brainwave binaural beats, to electronic, classical, modern day acoustic, or international flair, music is a powerful force in our lives. The scientific and evolutionary perspective of sound healing and sound therapy is powerful; some of your own playlists that you have created for your pleasure could work as part of your

EmotionalGRIT kit. Just as music can lift our spirits, it can lift levels of dopamine as well. Because dopamine regulates the anticipatory sectors of our brain, even the anticipation of hearing the music you want to hear can release dopamine and put your brain into a state of full awareness. Check out resources in back of the book for more brain-hacking beats.

Get hands-on

If you're anything like me, when I have the opportunity to work with my hands, I'm instantly calmer. Growing up cooking and playing the piano were activities that certainly sparked more creativity as well as creating more peace for me. Whether you like doing puzzles, cooking, gardening, auto-repair, drawing, or crafts, allowing your brain to work with your hands has a significant impact on dopamine levels. It's no wonder that coloring books have been such a huge hit in bookstores across the United States! Coloring is a therapeutic way to tap into creativity, single-focused tasks, and mindfulness—getting into the alpha state of calmness. Psychotherapist Lisa Assad Cates reports that these anxiety-relieving activities in our distraction-filled world offer a way to reconnect in establishing boundaries— in literally and figuratively coloring within the lines. What could be a better metaphor for creating better boundaries in work and life relationships. Not to mention, when you are engaging in more right-brained activities, you are strengthening different parts of your brain that (typically for those who are left-brained) signaling more of a response in the pre-frontal cortex to enhance creativity and a "flow" state. This also brings up the important reminder that if you are lacking a hobby—something that is *not* work-related and brings joy into your life—you may want to buy a coloring book!

Uplevel your nutrition

It's time to fully incorporate a few of the following foods in your daily diet. For example, increasing foods with probiotics (yogurt, pickled ethnic goods, kimchi, and kefir) and reducing sugar and bad fats from your diet can give the dopamine levels in your brain a double-punch of productivity. Choosing healthy fats like avocado, nuts, and eggs all can help your brain boost its power, keeping you on-task and allowing for better creativity and even joy in the mundane. Even making a small switch like replacing your breakfast of bread, juice, and coffee with a green juice smoothie with green tea, and vegetables makes a difference. Other good examples of simple switches to uplevel your optimal potential include selecting a few superfoods like turmeric, cinnamon, chia seeds, spirulina, chaga, reishi, matcha, and flaxeeds—just some of my personal favorites. (I have a list in the back of the book of foods to add to your daily regimen that can profoundly increase peak potential.)

The Power of Curiosity in Repetition

As overachievers and type-A dominated brains, you may want to avoid too much repetition. I'm people-motivated, instead of task-motivated (as many leaders are), so in trying to understand why in my youth I tended to shy away from repetitive tasks, I learned later it was because of a lack of curiosity. As a highly motivated learner, I always wanted to dig deeper and find out every single cause and effect from each situation I was experiencing. Non-repetitive learning was my preference because my brain favored stretching and growing. When I applied my innate human curiosity to repetition instead of being un-motivated to do certain tasks, I accomplished them with greater ease. Curiosity can have an extraordinary impact on how we approach tedious or tiresome tasks. Embracing curiosity has helped rediscover passion, hope, and possibility allowing the art of fun in even the most menial daily tasks.

In the era of tech and upgrading our own levels of reprogramming and "gamification," I believe that applying curiosity to tasks that you often don't choose first is a smart move as an entrepreneur, leader, or partner. In Erik Shonstrom's *Wild Curiosity*, he discusses the importance of approaching everyday problems with a healthy and curious mind. Shondstrom also discusses the importance of curiosity taught in schools; from the perspective as a parent, he watched his son navigate a tired school system void of the ability to not just instruct—but *teach and inspire* those that think or behave differently. He passionately explains that if we let go of how we once learned and to clear our slate and re-frame our mind that we would not only be more open to greater success, we would live more conscious and meaningful lives. Indeed, the entire focus of EmotionalGRIT is to work at becoming more empathetic leaders, and to do this, we must let go of the way we were born and raised—and learn a different way of living and leading. You are on the road to being boundless in exploration and discovery while dealing with the adversity and uncertainty that comes when things aren't in your control.

> It is the wisdom that persists as a result, and that is the essence of revolutionary emotional leadership.

There is a conscious duality of boundless curiosity and the discomfort of not knowing all of the answers, while being open to the experience of the situation or circumstance at hand. An example of this: An executive I was working with was undergoing a major merger and partner separation for a multi-million-dollar company. For his entire life, his strongest desire was significance and certainty; he thrived beautifully in business. However, internally, with these challenges that were outside of his "time" perception and control, it was eating him up inside. Constantly worried about the outside perception, family persona, and that he just couldn't get rid of this problem as fast as he wanted, he had no choice but to surrender in the day to day of unknowing. Gaining one of the single most transformative and resilient experiences of his life, he was able to reveal a more humbling and human side that was deathly afraid to emerge. The deep wisdom gained by simply leaning into the unknown with curiosity and without a resistance or fight makes the bumps along the way much smoother.

> The liberation is what sets you free from a society that places demands on us to obey.

Understanding and Implementing Boundaries

Cultivating curiosity and growth are also vital aspects in building and creating healthy boundaries for yourself and others around you. It is absolutely essential when growing to be willing to "protect" your time as a leader of your own life, and for the people that you are leading. Being able to create sustainable, healthy boundaries within relationships is key, and we need to learn to do so without the attachment to the guilt or anxiety and shame that can surface as a result.

This message is for those of you who grew up culturally with the construct that you pay respects to your elders, you don't talk back, everything that your parents say do and suggest is wholly and entirely correct and should never be challenged. As adults, the effect that this can have in the workplace and in our relationships is huge. You become people pleasers, only doing things and over doing to gain credibility and recognition in the eyes of parental and societal expectation. You consistently "feel bad," and in some parts of the world it's not even an option to commence difficult conversations for fear of letting down honor, legacy, family respect, and family name—and most of all, feeling deep guilt.

How does the lack of boundaries show up in the life you grow up to lead?

You begin to continue on this road of overworking, overcommitting, and overdoing without any regard or personal stand to put yourself, your desires and your needs as a priority. You can blame it on "working hard" or "climbing up the corporate ladder" —which can go on for a period of time until you face mental exhaustion or physical health scares. You allow relationships that are toxic into your life and friends that don't respect your time and take you for granted. Your love life attracts insecure partners to "test your love" but also to show and teach you to finally take a stand and declare what your wants, desires and needs are—and what your own beliefs and values are first.

Creating boundaries is difficult to teach because of the many layers of cultural complexities embedded for different people. During my Asia travels, I met a young woman who happened to be a 50-year-old generational heiress to the family's largest gem dealership in all of Thailand. In discovering her human dynamics with respect to her family, she told me she could never ever see herself ever mustering the courage or even the thought process to tell her father she wanted to live outside of the country and to do something completely different. She felt that the guilt of her forefathers having paved the way for an Ivy League education and her upbringing and lifestyle all were included in the price you pay for family sacrifice and continuing on the legacy. This is a prime example of deep roots of perception and awareness of the cultures of fear 'we've discussed already.

CHECK-IN

Analyzing your boundaries

To deconstruct this, here are the following steps to consider:

- Self-reflection: Are your boundaries being invaded? Do you have feelings of resentment, anger, or stress? Do you feel taken advantage of or as if your relationship is not respectfully mutual?

- Indentify the person: Is there a negative teammate, a demanding family member (mom guilt-trip effect) or a significant other/toxic friend/business partner who always makes you feel guilty?

- Make a list and write down the possible ways your boundaries have been invaded. The self-work you completed in chapter 4 on authenticity should help here. For those using the EmotionalGRIT guidebook, there are specific exercises to gain a deeper perspective. For example: what do you tolerate and what are your non-negotiables (punctuality, no calls after 10 pm, knock on your office door before entering, no meetings on Fridays): these are your own rules, and there's no right or wrong answer.

- What are the possible outcomes if you were to address your boundaries with this person? Having the awareness and deep understanding of the mindset of where the other person is operating from is key.

The goal here is to have the awareness that in even having this conversation you are taking one step in the right direction. Practice is important here. Mostly, being comfortable in knowing that if your boundaries have been invaded by these people for a while, they won't be expecting you to react or address them because you have never been firm on boundary creation in the first place. This may cause some initial discomfort, but go in knowing that you may experience major resistance and projecting from the other party—even them trying to push all of your previous triggers that previously would make you give in. Know and understand that this is bold. You are taking a stand, and protecting your values and your beliefs. You can be kind and firm at the same time, without needing to be afraid of hurting someone's feelings. This is the cornerstone of brilliantly successful people with high emotional intelligence.

Always wanting to try harder or achieve more, I allowed myself to have paper-thin or non-existent boundaries with people I loved because I was a big people-pleaser for most of my twenties. In cultivating a deeper understanding for the stories that we have and the perception that we carry from those around us, my fascination with human dynamics grew further. EmotionalGRIT was born out of my need to model and create empathetic leaders, while teaching and allowing others, especially from an ethnic background, that it is okay to set healthy boundaries. In fact, it's even more important to strengthen your own internal boundaries and not avoid confrontation, or ignoring the big elephant in the room and shoving these often large issues under a rug. You will avoid the inevitable passive-aggressive, resentful, and low energy level emotional states the more you practice.

> EmotionalGRIT was born out of my need to model and create empathetic leaders, while teaching and allowing others, especially from an ethnic background, that it is okay to set healthy boundaries.

On family boundaries

Starting with empathy can help boundaries and the psyche. Julie Hanks, a licensed clinical social worker in Salt Lake City, had a lot to say on boundaries. In a recent *Wall Street Journal* article, speaking with author Elizabeth Bernstein, she said, "Assume positive intent. The other person probably didn't mean to hurt or annoy you. A mother-in-law who drops by unannounced too often may miss her grandchildren and want a closer relationship with you." By focusing on the positive and not immediately jumping to the negative keeps your mind in the right frame of mind to question instead of condemn.

Even the most loving parent, the highest-performing CEO, or the most dutiful of employees has issues with healthy boundaries— simply because at the end of the day, we don't want to disappoint those that are the closest to us. At the GlobalGRIT institute, this happens to be the most common lecture and workshop I give when working with top leadership.

Remember: When we define ourselves based on and seek approval and validation in others, we compromise our self-worth as a result. We accommodate to their wants and their lifestyles, forgetting about our internal wants and desires. For you to become the best leader of your life, you must practice safe boundary creation from a place of guilt-free living. The following exercise will help you with boundaries and the "non-negotiable" aspects of your life.

So... now it's your turn. Time to check in.

- What are your boundaries?
- How have they been crossed in your personal lives or by your team members?
- Can you identify healthy boundaries with your team members?
- Is it possible to remember individuals that have crossed boundaries with you in the past?

List three potential ways you can strengthen these boundaries with the people that matter the most (and who often need boundaries drawn). For example: what are your non-negotiables; what will you not tolerate?

_____

_____

_____

_____

Take time to reflect on your emotions and hurtful things that have made you feel down or uneasy.

_____

_____

_____

_____

_____

In a few minutes, describe your must-haves for your personal space (home, office, etc.).

_____

_____

_____

_____

Do you have a personal value statement? List three things that are not allowed in any aspect of your life.

_____

_____

_____

_____

After defining the non-negotiable things that matter most to you, write down a time when each of these boundaries were violated. What did you do? How did you handle it? What would be a possible solution to handle it now?

_____

_____

_____

_____

_____

_____

_____

_____

_____

_____

_____

_____

_____

_____

GRIT perspectives on forgiveness and resilience

"I am constantly learning. We live in a world where people are scared to peg themselves into one category. They suffer paralysis by analysis thinking that once they choose a direction in life, they are stuck doing the same thing forever. It's completely the opposite! Life is a hallway filled with doors on either side- sometimes we will choose to enter one door and exit another. The BEST businesses in the world often do not end up doing what they started. Curiosity, transformation and innovation are what drive greatness." – Cameron Marawang, CEO and Forbes 30 under 30 Award Recipient

> *"I am the Queen of Google and curiosity, and before that-libraries and encyclopedias. Even as a child, if I saw something interesting, I would try to figure it out. What is it? How did they do that? I will try almost anything. I also look for ways to do things rather than assuming it's not feasible. (Often something is not possible, but I start with the default that it is and work from there.) I don't hope and dream. I do. A line from a speech I gave at a school: "I wasn't the type of little girl who dreamed of being a princess. I was the sort of kid who would try to figure out how to be a princess.... I have to marry a prince, so I need to find out what countries have them. This same trait led me into climbing. I didn't know outdoorsy people growing up. We never hiked, camped or fished. I had never been near a mountain nevertheless on one. That didn't stop me from signing up to backpack the New Hampshire Presidential Traverse (~25 miles across multiple peaks) the summer before college; or from convincing my best friend to learn to rock climb as a bonding trip before I moved to Japan; or from deciding to climb Rainier or Everest. Curiosity helped to find paths that I didn't know existed and to see that a lot more is possible than most people realize."* – Sofia Danenberg, First African-American to climb Mount Everest without a sherpa; TEDx speaker

Immediate Goal:

List 2 people this week that you will be practicing creating boundaries with. It can be loved ones, friends, or team members. Things to keep in mind: your conversation, your emotional awareness (what emotions/positive/negative come up when thinking about these individuals), and how will you do this (phone, in person, or email?).

<u>End-of-Chapter Exercise</u>

When is the last time you've allowed something NEW into your life? Whether a hobby, a class, or a new way of thinking or even travel, what have you done lately to inspire and practice curiosity in your life?

_____

_____

_____

_____

_____

_____

Setting healthy boundaries is one of many things you're learning in order to walk a healthier, happier path. One of the healthiest boundaries you can set is with yourself. What is one way you can set a boundary with yourself that will enhance your life?

_____

_____

_____

_____

_____

_____

_____

Recommended reading:

- *Wild Curiosity*, by Eric Shonstrom
- **The Heart and the Bottle**, by Oliver Jeffers
- *Blink: The Power of Thinking Without Thinking*, by Malcolm Gladwell
- *Boundaries: When to Say Yes, How to Say No, to Take Control of Your Life*, by Dr. Henry Cloud and Dr. John Townsend
- *Selfless Love*, by Ellen Jikai Birx

CHAPTER EIGHT

WHO IS IN CHARGE? YOU OR YOUR EGO?

"Be open and the world opens up to you." – Barack Obama

Chapter Intention: From this day forward, I will recognize my ego, and pay attention when it is driving, and when I need to partner up with it. I will not allow my ego to dictate my leadership, instead using it as a reminder that I am consistently doing the best that I can without disregarding those around me.

Chapter Checklist

- Understand how ego plays an essential role in your life as a leader.
- Determine when it is useful to practice self-awareness in moments of stressful periods when ego rises.
- Learn about cultivating self-compassion to "accept" and "understand" and appreciate both your strengths and shortcomings.
- Realize how your "past belief systems" have dictated your ego, how it plays a role in empathy and compassion in your own life.
- Learn how to finally break free from the expectations of society and quiet the sideline noise in embracing compassionate leadership.

The Problem of Ego

In this chapter you will learn how the cultures of fear drive the biggest dilemmas that we see in humanity today. You'll see how, on a global perspective, some of the leaders in our past have ruled based on ego, which at the basic core, is really only our self-protecting guard. Take for instance the war torn areas in various parts of the world, where the powers in leadership and control have caused division among their people, not to mention extreme massacres to human life every single day. Where the leaders in power were most likely governing from was a place of scarcity: "there isn't enough," so in turn we will do everything in our power to overprotect, control, and propel extreme dictatorship. While these are extreme examples, breaking it down for your own personal lives and the lives you lead becomes much simpler. The ego from an evolutionary perspective has been there to protect you as a shield when times are tough or when you are in danger. Now, when you take this from an individual level apply it to leader of a home, an organization, a Fortune 500 company, or a country, the lack of awareness around ego for that individual could have grave consequences for society in general.

Yet our desire for empathy in our leadership is on the rise. As a society, we have lived with the cultural divides formed by generations of fear-based leadership. For many, the new, desired form of leadership is based on conscious awareness.

In creating a new framework to challenge your beliefs and way of thinking, this is a means to harbor the thoughts, ideas and perspectives of a new frontier. We all need to reflect on inclusion, belonging, and bringing back the connectedness of humanity. This is why it's so important for you, individually, to understand the gravity of the turning point in the changing world of leadership today. Emotional leadership, which is simply being consciously aware of how you are showing up in the world every single day to those around you. It begins with going within your individual shell and practicing a deeper understanding of:

1. What is ego really?
2. How it can affect my decision-making?
3. What insecurities do I have that I use a mask to protect at times, since I am human?
4. Once aware, how can I be more empathetic to others and accept their perspective of the reasoning behind their actions.
5. How can I understand and practice non-judgement in the dynamics of others with their own protective mechanisms?
6. How can I be an example for others and understand to utilize my ego for good?

The background

Sigmund Freud famously said, "Groups take on the personality of the leader."

To Freud, this meant that individuals in leadership positions needed to have greater capacity for nurturing a positive environment. Freud also coined certain phrases about the human psyche, believing that individual personalities had more than one aspect. Freud believed there were three aspects to a psyche:

- ID (or IT): The primitive and instinctive component of personality.
- Ego: The primitive and instinctive component of personality.
- Superego: This incorporates the values and morals of society that are learned from one's parents and others.

Breaking it down on a human level, many philosophers, scientists, and behavior dynamics experts explain that ego is a guide for protection, i.e. if the ego was injured in the past or there was a trigger on the basis of the cultures of fear:

3 FEAR CULTURES

1 **CULTURE OF AVERSION**
"This isn't enough" so you do whatever it takes to avoid shame.

2 **CULTURE OF SCARCITY**
"There isn't enough" so you become hypercompetitive, over protective/selfish.

3 **UNWORTHINESS**
"I'm not enough" so self-acceptance becomes conditional; failure will happen, since expectations can never be met.

When we feel like our resources are in danger, the innate human behavior response is to protect ourselves, often by engaging a fear response.

When you understand that your ego is your intermediary in conflicts with everyone from friends, to business partners, you can develop a clearer path to negotiating between your desire to protect yourself and other people's needs.

From a scientific and neurological approach, you have already learned that on a cellular level, your brain prepares you for imminent danger by setting off stress chemicals throughout your body (increasing the production of cortisol, the stress hormone in the flight/fight response), which thereby shuts down curiosity and higher levels of creative thinking which makes it difficult to make sound judgements not based on fear. This is because your body is trying to protect you. Now, your ego does the exact same thing, offering protection.

How you navigate your ego will be your internal guide in revealing the better parts of yourself that have yet to emerge.

<u>Check-in</u>:

What the GlobalGRIT Institute uses to assess ego in leadership.

This is a great assessment tool that you can share and use as a framework and as a radar.

1. Do you get offended? (If so, when, why and how?)
2. Do you always need to win?
3. Do you constantly need to be right? (why?)
4. Do you find yourself wanting to constantly be the best or the greatest?
5. Do you find yourself always needing more; are you never satisfied?
6. Do you need to identify yourself based on what you've done? (Do you need to showcase your accolades, boast about your degrees, accomplishments)
7. Do you worry about your reputation constantly, and are you defined by it?

Do you always need to have the last word?

When ego can work for you

By the same token, there are many reasons why ego is often a great tool. With communication styles between men and women, men are more likely to use their ego in decision-making and show self-confidence and self-awareness. In starting a business, organization, and even promoting yourself to the world, your ego needs to be solid and firm on steady ground in order to gain the recognition, respect, and credibility of those you wish to interact with, hire, do business with, and more.

In interviewing investors on how ego plays a role in decision-making, Matt McCall from the Pritzker Group, who has backed many key entrepreneurs such as Elon Musk, illustrates that as a venture capitalist, your goal is to make sure your bets will be creating long-term and sustainable impact. Although VCs can often get a bad rap as being ego-driven (*Shark Tank* is an example), he believes, as a former columnist for *Forbes*, that venture capital is a huge platform for good, creating entrepreneurship opportunities for those keen on sharing their gifts with the world. Yet, when pitching ideas to investors, especially when you are not entirely sure of the valuation of your company, you need to partner up with your ego and realize the positioning that you need to push your ideas forward and inspire people and teams to galvanize around you.

What's a leader to do? It's important to keep your ego in-check and practice the steps of emotional leadership and your EmotionalGRIT. While the foundation lies in the characteristic of authenticity, it is non-negotiable to b be truthful and honest in your communication style, conveying what you deem is important. With all of the practice from the exercises in the previous chapters, you should have a better handle on this. Have the courage to practice your boundaries. Embrace your natural curiosity to hear and understand another person's thought process. Accept and appreciate the different perspectives of those around you (especially those on your team and business). All of these tools boost your emotional leadership intelligence to your team and organization.

This system of acceptance and awareness, as Daniel Goleman, pioneer of the emotional intelligence movement, has defined them, are the first steps in being able to cultivate openness and empathy-based leadership.

Here are a few ways to keep a healthy balance in your ego that will help your team and company:

- **Develop a life of inclusion by inviting many different individuals to your table.** Taking time to recognize the individuality of those around you will help you to have a community of contributors that feel valued. By having strong diversity of thought, creativity and wisdom, you'll see more new ways of tackling projects and thinking through challenges than ever before. You'll also foster a culture of learning and acceptance, which is where innovation thrives!

- **Appreciate what you don't understand.** Have you ever gone around a slow driver in the left lane to see a parent struggling with children in the backseat? Perhaps you waited oh-so-patiently at the drive-through while someone took their time with pennies, nickels and dimes. We know nothing of what others are facing in their lives if we don't ask. I've tried to develop a true sense of appreciation for people, situations, and moments of frustration. That tests your truest form of EmotionalGRIT. My new-found awareness to my own triggers has brought about a grateful attitude has helped keep me calmer and humbler in stressful situations that are often out of your control.

- **Ask for feedback and be open to listen.** Asking for feedback is one way to show you are actively listening and want to include those around you. **Not jumping to the defensive when you hear feedback dictates how great a leader you can be.** This is the hallmark of building your emotional endurance muscle. This is wildly important. Even if you don't agree with the feedback, try and ask open-ended questions to find out where the individual's reasoning is coming from; you might be surprised by the answer.

2 minute EGO Self-Defense -check-in- Rising tension-

So, someone has challenged you. They don't agree with what you are saying. They vehemently turn down your point of you, and you feel everything inside of your core being begin to tense. Physically, your heart rate may start to beat fast, your eyes may grow wider, and your nose may start to flare. Essentially ready for verbal combat, or also known as your "guards" are now up— time to defend myself and my opinions.

1. What are you feeling? What triggers are coming up? (attacked, threatened, not prepared, inadequate?)
2. What negative emotions (from the list in the back of the book) are you experiencing right now?
3. Who is the person that is causing you to experience this tension? How often are these 'buttons' or triggers' being signaled (it's almost often the closest people in your life).
4. Take 3 deep belly breaths before responding. Think from the above EGO assessment checklist- which one do you feel the need to prove/use?
5. Finally, take the perspective of the person giving the opinion and their perception or the 'why' behind their thought process.
6. Do you still wish to respond as a reaction, or rather from a place of a curious solution seeker?

An ego is an important part of your personality, but not THE most important part. By recognizing your mind's need for an ego—and not allowing it to rule your decisions, behavior, and actions—you're growing the muscle in strengthening your emotional leadership skills.

EGO CHECK IN

1   Do you get offended? (when, why and how)

2   Do you always need to win?

3   Do you constantly need to be right? (why)

4   Do you find yourself wanting to constantly be the best or the greatest?

5   Do you find yourself always needing more; are you never satisfied?

6   Do you need to identify yourself based on what you've done? (showcase your accolades)

7   Do you worry about your reputation constantly, and are you defined by it?

8   Do you always need to have the last word?

Using your ego for good

Wayne Dyer is one of my favorite writers and speakers. He once said, "When your ego shows up trying to make you doubtful, fearful or unsure about the choices you make, these ego-friendly principles will clear the cobwebs, empower you and reveal your true self." He also has a few fantastic ideas on not allowing your ego to control your life, or as I call it, "using your ego for good."

Here are three great ways to let your ego bring out the positive in yourself and those around you:

1. Let go of your need to win.
2. Create and stay true to your core values, your belief systems that shape you.
3. Let go of the need to be right.

To explain further:

- **Let the game go**. Ego loves to divide us up into winners and losers. As humans, it is our natural reaction to want to win. Our brains release the hormone dopamine which is the "good feeling" when this happens. This is why competition can be addicting. However, it is absolutely impossible to lead your life this way. Truth be told: there will always be someone more successful, more attractive, more fit, better, and faster than you. Chasing these unreasonable expectations only leaves you continuously feeling inadequate, insignificant, and always having to "keep up" with the competition—and unfortunately will leave you to feel you will never be good enough.
- **Authentic Vision**. Living authentically allows you to architect your own reality, based on your terms. When you quiet the sideline noise of "who is saying what, or doing what" it is much easier to pursue the unique gift you wish to add to the world with passion. Essentially, your purpose should be to keep pushing toward that goal, no matter what externally shakes you. Many of us don't operate this way. If your core values are not solid, you will be easily influenced, self-doubting, comparing, and wavering, sending your ego into a downward spiral.
- **Let go of your need to be right.** This is instant validation. Ego can be the source of tension, communication stressors, and conflict. Whether you are an authority of your household or your business, it pushes you in the direction of making other people wrong. When the focus is on being right and proving your point, it often becomes more about the situation itself increasing the tension, creating a brewing pot of hostility resulting in a cuisine laden with anger, resentment, and no proper solutions. Being aware of your EmotionalGRIT in this

process in responding with characteristics such as compassion and curiosity is much better recipe for success.

- **Your reputation does not define you.** Go ahead and repeat that. The perceptions, and thoughts of other people belong to others. You will never be able to have control over that. So, it's time to let that go. As heart centered humans, once you are elevating your framework of thinking, and mindset- you are more equipped with the tools to understand that we are all similar. We all have shared desires, and shared fears. Masks and shields to protect this can often arise. The goal is to become aware of this and focus on your strengths, your unique gifts which then help to quite the sideline noise. Your ego will be there to challenge that. Yet, it is your responsibility in these critical moments to decide how the external noise affects your inner strength. It is foolish to waste your energy and time to win the validation or approval of the hearts of others. As Wayne Dyer says in *The Power of Intention*, "Stay on purpose, detach from outcome, and take responsibility for what *does* reside in you: your character. Leave your reputation for others to debate; it has nothing to do with you."

- **Who's judging, anyway?** Our ego likes to size up ourselves to others. Comparing your ability to achieve, accomplish, which is straining and stressful and not to mention exhausting. As humans, you enter a new meeting, an unfamiliar place, or particular group of new people- it is your innate ability to scan the crowd and judge. Noticing that your ego has its protective guards around you. When you are being open and unafraid you are able to have better conversations, and lead better when you are coming from a place of kindness rather than fear and judgment.

- **Be bravely courageous**. Imposter syndrome, self-critique, and self-doubt will show up. Ego protects us from feeling fear and our most intimate and scariest insecurities. Your responsibility as emotionally intelligent leaders is to be aware of this. It is powerful. When you understand that it's your ego saying hello, you can practice more self-compassion and being brave in facing your fears head first instead of allowing your ego to place that big giant wall of protection.

> "Courage is not the absence of fear; it is taking action despite fear. When faced with doubt and insecurities, resolve to be courageous and take the risk to do the thing that has you stuck in fear." – Franklin Roosevelt

The power of positive thinking and positive psychology in action

Do you know someone who is always positive, an eternal optimist of sorts? While many individuals find Freud's concepts dated, I believe he hit the nail on the proverbial head with his thoughts around positive thinking. Did you know that Robert Noyce, Intel co-founder, once said that "optimism is an essential ingredient of innovation?" Those that feature optimism as a part of their lives, listen for what is RIGHT in what those around them are saying, while pessimists look to "de-bunk" or prove wrong what's being said. Perhaps you can practice what you have been learning on the EmotionalGRIT journey here. Do you see the tie-in with what we just talked about above? An ego can act like a pessimist in many situations—and it's important to keep it in-check! It could also reveal an underlying need to be in control, and goes back to earlier chapters in laying down the values of where 'certainty' or the need to feel safe plays a role in your decision making. Is it beginning to make sense? I believe and celebrate in the power of optimists, every day.

Not only are optimists greater innovators, they often take more risks and are willing to stand up for their idea, or product while others are not quite ready to get on-board. Emotionally intelligent leaders are optimistic within their framework of thinking. They realize and understand the behavior dynamics of others around them, don't take the perspective of others personally, and can communicate effectively. without their ego in the driver's seat. One of the key EmotionalGRIT characteristics is the attitude which is important in maintaining your optimism even when your ego challenges you.

Do you avoid confrontation?

Would you like to just pretend that the problem would just go away? That the other person will just automatically know how they have hurt you (or vice versa)? Difficult conversations are ticking time bombs to some—but they don't have to be. Begin with shifting your thought process. Understanding the idea of having a courageous conversation instead. When we let stressful thoughts around conversations that *should* take place fester, they eat at the core of who we are. Then, resentment builds towards the other person. This is one reason why workplaces can get toxic very, very quickly. Let's face it. It is much easier to avoid conflict, bring up a situation that doesn't sit well with you, perhaps makes you feel uneasy, and you think (or desperately wish) it will disappear or resolve itself overtime. Bad idea. As humans, we have a strong desire to communicate. Even the most effective leaders need to practice their emotional health through effective communication techniques. In times of crisis, keep these three things in mind:

- Start by complimenting the person, acknowledging their presence and worth.
- Identify the situation, present the facts, and share why you feel the way you do. Be sure to come from a place of curiosity and concern, not anger or resentment.
- Listen to their side of the story, and find a way ask to come to a mutually beneficial outcome, deadline, or agreement. Ending things on a positive note will help you feel better about taking on this tough task.

I often sit down with leaders and role-play, giving those I talk to the opportunity to deliver difficult news or start a stressful conversation. A typical script for starting any difficult conversation should start like this:

"Name, thank you for taking time out of your day to sit down with me. I really value your input regarding _____. Here's the situation, I'd really appreciate your thoughts..."

Do you see how this method immediately unarms the other person across the table? They are no doubt just as concerned about this conversation as you are, but by taking their emotions into account, you're showing them that not only is this a safe place to communicate, but that as a leader, you are open and ready for their feedback.

<u>Courageous Conversations</u>

Here's an exercise to get you started:

Tomorrow you are going to tackle a conversation you've been putting off. What are the first two sentences you'll say to disarm the other person or persons, and help the conversation start in the best possible way? Write them out below:

_____

_____

_____

_____

_____

_____

Next, I want you to share how you THINK the conversation will go. What do you think will happen? Give some insight here:

_____

_____

_____

_____

_____

_____

By doing the above, you are practicing thoughtful, compassionate leadership—and it doesn't even have to be in a workplace setting! Did you know that some experts believe that this new model of compassion is fueling the economy?

PBS recently aired a report asking the question, "Is there a connection between prosperity, compassion and happiness?" Their findings seem to back up exactly what others have known for a while. During a Q&A on PBS' report, Dacher Keltner at the University of California, Berkeley found the following,

> *"What we have learned from really interesting neuroscience is that humans, in the face of threat, connect to other people. And then complementarily, if you grow up in a more privileged circumstance, you orient inwards to what's inside of you. And those are two fundamentally different ways of approaching the world."*

Based on Keltner's work, it was found that lower-income subjects not only reported more compassion, their vital signs indicated they really meant it, especially their slower heart rates. When we think of compassion, we typically think of individuals who specialize in philanthropy, with millions of dollars at their disposal, like the Gates Foundation. What's so interesting about Keltner's study is that it proves that compassion—real compassion—can come from the most unlikely of sources.

The Economics of Compassion

Many companies like Caring Economics, an initiative born out of the Max Planck Institute of Human, Cognitive and Brain Sciences, have always known that compassion is tied to economy. In fact, as a team member of Caring Economics, Tania Singer, a Director of the Department of Social Neuroscience at the Max Planck Institute for Human Cognitive and Brain Sciences in Leipzig, has been named one of the most influential women in the economy. In recent research, Singer found that empathy lit up the brain alike to painful experiences. Singer believes that if people could attain compassionate states, it would have a direct impact on the economy.

She states:

> *"Empathy is quite generally the ability to share feelings with others: when you, for example, are hurt, or worried, or afraid, and I am standing there, then I as an empathetic human experience negative feelings as well. Such affective resonance is practically universal: pretty much everybody does it... Compassion, on the other hand, is a reaction to another's suffering from an entirely different world. We can verify this through brain physiology: when somebody is in pain, a compassionate reaction does not replicate the painful state itself, but rather produces feelings of concern and warmth as well as a motivation to help the sufferer."*

Singer isn't alone in her research. Dan Waldschmidt, a well-known speaker and researcher, believes that compassion and "love economies" drive significant sales. Here's what he thinks (and I agree!):

> *"The current selling environment lacks the tolerance for product pitches. It's all about people pitches. It's actually always been about people, but limited access to data has historically allowed sellers to create thriving businesses around product superiority. Those days are past. You now need to obsess about the buyer. And when you love, you can't help but keep the buyer squarely in your sights. It's inevitable that your kindness builds outrageous success."*

Waldschmidt knows what good salespeople have known all along: that a strong EQ and empathy can help turn "I'm not sure" into "Yes!" INC Magazine suggested in a 2016 article that empathy-based writing could be as much as three times more effective. "Empathy puts our brains into the right frame of mind to be sold to," INC explained. "It's the basis of the Problem-Agitator-Solution formula that copywriters use for sales writing. Find a problem, stir

178

up the negative emotions associated with it, and then present a simple, easy solution."

Writing, speaking, and leading all have it covered: empathy wins.

It's final: we're hardwired for compassion

Dr. James Doty, the author of *The Science of Compassion*, recently attended the Templeton Prize Ceremony in London. He has spent many years researching the impact compassion has on our ego, brain, and body. After reflecting on the Dalai Lama's words, he also found that compassion must be tied to a direct effect for people to listen. The Dalai Lama explained, "If we say, oh, the practice of compassion is something holy, nobody will listen. If we say, warm-heartedness really reduces your blood pressure, your anxiety, your stress and improves your health, then people pay attention."

In Chapter 2, I showed you the benefits of EQ as well as empathy. Compassion can help our world and our lives—but only if we listen. I believe the world is suffering from a self-inflicted pain, one that can be ended if we so choose. The answer is simple: *Connectedness*. Human connectedness is the understanding that with compassion we realize we all have desires, wants, fears, and insecurities—all of the essences that make us real, raw, and human. Yet without it, we tend to be fearful in our decision-making. We are not quite open to understanding the perspectives of others, judgmental and emotionally unavailable resulting in even more barriers, and ultimately leads to our inability to chart forward- causing a stunted growth in our evolution.

> *"Compassion is an instinct. Recent research shows that even animals such as rats and monkeys will go through tremendous effort and cost to help out another of its species who is suffering. We human beings are even more instinctually compassionate; our brains are wired for compassion."* – Dr. James Doty, Director of the Center for

Compassion and Altruism Research and Education (CCARE) at Stanford University.

Using empathy in your life

Now that you are exhibiting self-awareness, you can understand the process underlining your past belief systems and use them to build on assessing and understanding your ego. This will also help you learn how your ego plays a role in empathy and compassion in every aspect of your life. In fact, by using self-compassion to accept and understand the GRIT process, you allow your strengths to shine past your shortcomings.

GRIT perspectives on ego

"I see the GRIT key drivers of resilience and authenticity in my life and business. I started a company that weathered the last economic downturn. We had to reshape the business in reaction to tough times and pivoted to new business models. While working in the entertainment industry, you see so many that 'talk a big game' or promise much and never deliver. Sometimes the ego can get the best of you especially when working with big talent. Trusting my instincts, I was able to bring the first global talent from Bollywood to the U.S. and that has proven to show great growth during this season. Priyanka Chopra has not only transcended my vision, but exceeded expectations to open up doors for other South Asian talent making their way into the U.S. market. I always wanted to inject authenticity in the way I conduct business and be true to my word." – Ranj Bath, Serial Entrepreneur, Investor

"I started the world's first inspirational platform, connecting all entrepreneurs, without the typical constructs of a conference setting. This allowed for more collaboration, and true connection. I realized through making a list of all the items I hated, that leadership is allowing other people to make decisions. The genius of my model is helping to empower people all over the globe to make their own decisions; creating a container for a new reality, error, humility and getting sh*t done." – Jonathan Lewis, Author, Professor Entrepreneurship, Social Entrepreneurship Director- NYU, Director/Founder Opportunity Collaboration

Immediate Goal

- This EmotionalGRIT stage is all about committing yourself to meaningful change, challenging your ego and re-defining your leadership style. To do all of these, you must begin with empathy and compassion. In what ways can you be adding more empathy and compassion this week?

__End-of Chapter-Exercise__

Whether at work or our home, the ego tends to be triggered when we feel "less than." What are some things you can do when you recognize your ego is taking over?

_____

_____

_____

_____

_____

Compassion is steps to shift the ego. In leading with compassion and empathy, you are able to practice understanding the different perspectives of the humans around you. Can you identify three to five situations in your everyday life where you can put compassion before ego?

_____

_____

_____

_____

_____

<u>Recommended reading:</u>

o   ***The Void: Inner Spaciousness and Ego Structure***, by A.H. Almaas
o   ***Gilead: A Novel***, by Marilynne Robinson
o   ***Nothing Special***, by Charlotte J. Beck and Steve Smith
o   ***The Ego Tunnel: The Science of the Mind and the Myth of the Self***, by Thomas Metzinger

CHAPTER NINE

FORGIVE, LET GO, AND REDEFINE YOUR IDENTITY

"The season of failure is the best time for sowing the seeds of success." – Yogananda

Chapter Intention: I am taking an important step today, releasing myself from being too self-critical, and practicing self-compassion and self-acceptance. Today, I realize that I'm doing the best that I can. I set forth to practice better discernment in my judgment and know that the decisions that I make are simply part of my learning experience. Forgiving myself first is key.

Chapter Checklist

- Gain perspective on the attachment theory
- Understand imposter syndrome, so that you can avoid mental burnout and navigate your internal framework
- Learn to practice self-compassion and release being self-critical to prepare yourself for compassionate leadership and create your new identity. Recognize your gifts so you can share them unapologetically with the world.

Imposter Syndrome

We're about to tackle something faced by many CEOs with whom I work: Imposter syndrome.

In becoming more emotionally intelligent, this is something many suffer from in silence. In interviews with leaders from all sectors, from startup founders to doctors to billionaires, imposter syndrome is something that isn't brought into light simply because of the shame around it. As a leader, as you learned in the last chapter, the ego definitely will want to protect and hide this. Yet it is essential for you in becoming more emotionally aware that this is in fact a common feeling.

This term was first used in 1978 by clinical psychologists Dr. Pauline R. Clance and Suzanne A. Imes. It refers to high-achieving individuals who are unable to believe in their own worth or accomplishments, instead believing they are a "fraud."

Sometimes we believe we need "permission" for the silliest of things: happiness, following our dreams or taking a new job. For example, imagine the lives of some of the most famous icons in history. Consider the global sensation and musical genius of Michael Jackson. Making music at a young age and growing up on stage, for Jackson, of course, insecurities and self-doubt would rise to the top. Or, we examine the case of Facebook CEO Mark Zuckerberg: a tech luminary and overnight success who changed the way we communicate. He may epitomize strength, yet behind the veneer he projects to the world, he too experiences the inevitable pressure to work harder to keep up with his persona. Naturally, as a leader, it is important to be aware of these emotions and how they may be taking their toll.

Understanding that as you rise in your respective business, craft, career, or overall impact in the world- thinking that someone will "figure you out" is a problem that many leaders, CEOS and professionals that I interact with face every day. Feeling that you are an "imposter" that you don't deserve to be in the place that you are in, perhaps you may experience self-doubt, self-critique of thinking that I just got "lucky" or I haven't been doing "X" long enough- it can have a grave toll on your psyche and spill over into other aspects of your life.

GoodStartups CEO Justin Milano created a program called "Breakthrough Fear Curriculum" that specifically addresses this dilemma, which runs rampant in the Silicon Valley startup entrepreneurial scene, where, on average, 95% of startups will fail. The program is geared towards educating venture capitalists to foster proper education and emotional intelligence support for hungry tech stars not just to help them grow resilience, but as a means of protecting their assets.

It is interesting to note that imposter syndrome could evolve the practice of constantly measuring ourselves up to those around us, that ultimately you are just "not good enough". We ask deeper inherent questions of self-worth, and in a phenomena known as "fear patterning," we work harder, overachieve and overdo as a result to keep up with the demands or the "brilliance" around us.

Maya Angelou, the international beacon of inspiration and well-known author and speaker, silently struggled with imposter syndrome.

> "I have written 11 books, but each time I think, 'Uh oh, they're going to find out now. I've run a game on everybody, and they're going to find me out."

Overcoming the feeling of being an imposter

So, how do you overcome something that consistently challenges and pokes holes in your self-worth? First, you allow yourself to understand your emotions and which part of your old "story" is coming up. What fear is it pointing to? Is it something that a former boss, teacher, or friend said to you at some point in the past that you haven't been able to let go?

In dental school I experienced this almost daily and excruciatingly. I remember that all 150 of us were high achievers, all of us products of a straight A, goal-oriented culture. We had made it through an application pool of 5,000 for the University of Illinois in Chicago, so the pressure was really on! Coupled with this: the profession was now allowing more women into dental school, so the pressures and stakes were high to prove that you were worthy to have a spot in the clinic.

In this profession, we all learned quickly that you were validated for your "right" memorized answers. always felt the urge to spit out facts like an encyclopedia, truly preventing me from being authentic. This also placed grave harm on how I would interact in open symposium discussions. I was deathly afraid to utter a word for this exact fear: imposter syndrome.

Forbes journalist Margie Warrell says it best: "Overcoming the Imposter Syndrome requires self-acceptance: you don't have to attain perfection or mastery to be worthy of the success you've achieved and any accolades you earn along the way. It's not about lowering the bar, it's about resetting it to a realistic level that doesn't leave you forever striving and feeling inadequate. You don't have to be Einstein to be a valuable asset to your organization and to those around you. Nor do you have to attain perfection to share something with the world that enriches people's lives in some way."

> "You don't have to attain perfection or mastery to be worthy of the success you've achieved."
> – Margie Warrell

In the GRIT process, the first step toward combating imposter syndrome is self-awareness, part of the **GROW** process.

- Reflect on your feelings of self-worth and notice which emotional triggers arise. Where do negative feelings associated with imposter syndrome, pop up?
- Next comes the second step in EmotionalGrit: **Reveal**. Come to terms with the self-acceptance that you are doing the best that you can. You'll gain perspective when you understand that you are sharing your unique gifts in the world at the highest level (assuming that you've identified and embraced your strengths).
- That's when you are able to notice, as a third party viewing yourself, that it's simply your ego protecting you from your previous cultures of fear.
- Wave to it, embrace the feeling, honor it—and let it .go.

Can self-critique limit your abilities to be extraordinary in other areas of your life, especially your relationships with your family, and even a partner in love? Absolutely. It could also prove to be detrimental, preventing you from being fully truthful and honest in your relationships, consistently thinking about the possibility of being a "fraud." Thoughts like "I am not good enough" or "my children won't like me" can take over. You may be tempted to overcompensate by "buying" affection, or to succumb to jealous or overprotective thoughts.

Attachment theory

We must also consider the idea of where we attach our self-worth.

Attachment theory stems from John Bowlby's work in analyzing the interpersonal dynamics in humans, and was further adapted into romantic relationships in adults by social psychologists Cindy Hazen and Phillip Shiver. Essentially, at the psychological level, it speaks to how humans react within relationships when experiencing hurt, loss or separation from loved ones, or anxiety:

1. **Secure attachment**: correlates to healthy and positive views of oneself.
2. **Anxious-ambivalent attachment**: often seeks high levels of intimacy and approval from partners, becoming highly over-dependent and are usually less trusting and have low self-worth.
3. **Dismissive-avoidant attachment**: are fully unattached, avoid vulnerability in relationships, and require a strong level of independence. Are self-sufficient and usually deal with rejection by distancing themselves from their partners.
4. **Fearful-avoidant attachment**: has mixed feelings wanting closeness, yet are fearful of becoming attached. This group tends to mistrust their partners believing they are unworthy, and typically suppress their feelings.

Depending on attachment style, the person with imposter syndrome will then attribute all of their success to luck and will continuously believe they are unworthy. But there are others who attribute their success to hard work and perseverance, according to the study done by Shohreh Ghorbanshirodi in studying emotional intelligence and imposter syndrome in medical students.

As you may have guessed, depending on your attachment style, you can definitely bring stories from your past into your interpersonal relationships. Emotional triggers may show up as challenges in the workplace or other relationships, as old childhood wounds can reveal themselves unexpectedly. Facing these issues is your opportunity to seize your emotional intelligence and begin to create a new identity. There's a solution to combat imposter syndrome: Self-compassion.

Now it's your turn.

Take a few moments to pause and think about what your attachment style has been. How has it affected some of the personal life decisions that you have made? Have you ever hung on to a relationship, even though it was toxic? Have you avoided your family life entirely because you feel that they have let you down? Give yourself some time, and book mark this page to come back to it and reflect. This is wildly important because once you have a deep understanding of this you can move into your professional and career world. Within certain business decisions, financial decisions and motivations that play an integral role in your leadership, this also can play a role. Reflect on the partnerships that have gone good or bad, or even that one time when you invested or were afraid to fully commit 100% what attachment style and fear culture played a role? Essentially peeling away some of those layers gears you up for the next steps ahead.

The greatest good: self-compassion

The world is rising with more compassion. A few years ago I attended an experience that forever changed my life. It was my first experience of a "collective effervescence" former Airbnb executive Chip Conley describes as he sits on the board of a week-long festival celebrating humanity called Burning Man. In the simplest terms, it's a gathering of people from around the world the size of a small city, transforming the desert into one of the world's greatest displays of collaborative, supportive, and compassionately heart-centered individuals. From thought leaders, executives, government officials, families, as well as futurists, innovators, creative specialists, humanists, it is the sum display of Ted-style talks, showcasing some of the most expansive art and out of the box concepts in a vast open landscape. Where the principles include full inclusion, celebration of uniqueness, the artists were in charge, and love was the only currency. This was the first time I experienced full self-compassion as well as what a sliver of what is possible when hundreds of thousands of others govern with that same type of perspective and lens.

There was no judgment, no fear. For seven days a collective and supportive utopian community formed, where curiosity and inquisitiveness sparked deep conversation. Egos are put to the side and ideas are brought to life. From problem solving, to business strategizing; startups form, companies unite, and a tight bond is created out of a human experience that connects people through authentic relationships and vulnerability. It's no wonder that when fears are put away, as it happens at Burning Man, innovative ideas emerge.

When you are able to practice more self-compassion, it begins to spill into the lives that you touch. That is the beginning of charting your new identity. It's ready to emerge into the world.

Here are five ideas to instill self-compassion in yourself in the most surprising of ways:

1. **Forgive Your Past.** Forgiveness liberates and gives you the freedom to close chapters in your life. By taking time to forgive the past, you literally close the seasons in your life (whether projects, businesses, people, relationships, or team members). Practicing forgiveness allows you to let in other fresh, innovative opportunities for the potential to grow as a better leader in your life.

2. **Take time to de-clutter.** Another way to practice self-compassion is to create work or life spaces that allow innovation and peace. In Ari Meisel's book *Less Doing* he points out how important it is to de-clutter our lives, prioritizing the things we want to do, and outsourcing the things we don't have to do. A friend of mine calls this, "Delegate and Elevate!"

3. **Start with an inventory of your week.** It is so important to dissect the 24 hours that you have daily so that you can make the most of the things you WANT to be spending your time doing.

4. **Delegate and let go.** Investigate how much time you'll save by delegating items that you can. As Ari mentions in his book, you learn a tremendous amount about yourself in the process and how effective your communication is. A few of my favorite websites for this are Fancyhands.com, elance.com, and taskrabbit.com.

5. **Take mini breaks during the day.** Many life hacking/production experts say break your day up. If your day is too crammed for yoga or a workout, take five-to-ten minutes at the end of each hour to get up stretch your legs. Most importantly, take three deep breaths to give your body the ability to have a restful moment.

The future awaits for compassionate leaders

The Dalai Lama's 80th birthday wish was a global movement for all to live by: #withcompassion. When you open the floodgates to compassion, your fear guards are easily broken and you lead from a place of respect, harmony, and genuine care for the people that you serve and the relationships you are building.

This in turn builds lasting relationships and trust, which is the future of the new economy. For businesses, rather than the antiquated fear-based model, the key is being less about "you" and your interpersonal insecurities, but rather how you will share and bring to light your genuine gifts in the world. Without any shame, fear, or judgment that you aren't good enough, you aren't perfect enough, or that you are not worthy.

"Every human being has the same potential for compassion; the only question is whether we really take any care of that potential, and develop and implement it in our daily life" – The Dalai Lama

Your new identity awaits, and it's one filled with many of the characteristics it takes for revolutionary leadership, for shifting the stories, growing compassion, and seeding it into every relationship and person that you meet.

GRIT perspectives on self-compassion

"I grew up around artists, and I had a belief that my singing and performing wasn't ever good enough. I absolutely loved performing, but had extraordinary standards for myself since my mother was a music teacher. It wasn't until I was surrounded by my supportive community and realized that music was healing, and opened up the often-buttoned up CEOs allowing them the opportunity to play. Yet because of growing up with a singing and songwriting mother as a music teacher, it limited my thinking of the music that I would create, thinking that it was never good enough. Thinking that my voice wasn't as good as my mother's. Through instances of my own self-discovery, I developed an international platform to teach others to free their voice, a combination of a "songversation": a monologue, performance and show which has led me to perform at places like Richard Branson's Necker Island. Letting go is a big part to watch your journey unfold." – Jess Johnson, Singer, Heartist, Songwriter

"Things changed for when I learned how to let go a little bit and also let some things happen instead of controlling everything. Being diagnosed with cancer at the age of 20 a few months before my traditional Indian parents wanted me to get married, I decided to undergo chemotherapy. Then I told my mother that for an aviation industry that is dominated by all men, I was set out to disrupt it. With self-compassion and drive, I told my mother that within 5 years I would be in the Forbes magazine. – Kanika Tekriwal, Forbes 30 under 30, CEO JetSetGo

"On a beautiful Friday afternoon while walking down Shattuck Avenue in Berkeley, my cell phone began to ring. To my delightful surprise, it was my mother! At this point in my life after years of ups and downs, I enjoyed having my mother call. She called me often to keep me up to date on family affairs, grandchildren being born and getting married. Being one of twelve children and having around seventy nieces and nephews, she was calling me quite frequently. But this time there was something different in her voice, and I couldn't make out what it was. She proceeded to ask me, "Kalmy, I would like you to go sit down for a minute." Perplexed and unsure of why she wanted me to do that, I told her to give me a minute so I could situate myself in the café I was standing nearby. "Okay, Mother. I am sitting," I said, while wondering what is that important and dramatic that requires me to sit. "You know that your sister is at the age that she needs to find the right boy to get married to, right?" "Yes..." Still confused since good news should be coming... "Kalmy, if you are not okay with it, I will never question your decision. If you don't feel right with it, I will completely understand and never hold it against you. Three different Shadchunim (matchmakers) have independently recommended this very nice boy for your sister, but your father and I didn't even want to consider it before asking you." ... I was still a bit confused. "If you found the right match for my youngest sister why are you asking me for permission?" I thought to myself. She then went on to tell me, "He is the son of your abuser." This is the man who had sexually abused me and countless of other children in a span of three decades. And just like that, I blessed the matchmaking of my sister. The very fact that my mother would consider my input, given my experience, was such a healing moment for me. It was one of those indirect validations of my parents acknowledging my past pain and abuse that was not spoken about for many years. This moment proved to myself my *emotional maturity and how far I had come since childhood. I was able to have enough intelligence to look at the situation and not perpetuate suffering.*

Saying "yes" to my mother and giving my blessing to the marriage led me to start my organization that would introduce a new conversation around sexual trauma. I was done holding back my silence and needed to be the strength that other people didn't have. I came back to the community and saw that after years of being gone, the same abuse was continuing and nothing had changed. From that moment, I was inspired to start my non-profit organization which would run programs in educating the community on how to end the cycle of sexual abuse and have a better understanding of the impact it has on children. This experience has taught me many things, one being true satisfaction comes when I choose not to be a bystander, but to take an active role in creating change, especially in the areas that are within my reach to do so.

This was the start of something really beautiful. My relationship with my family changed from that moment on. My mother was more vulnerable with me, I was able to open up to her further, it lead to others sharing similar stories in the community, and eventually helped launch programs to help people recover and find hope again. I couldn't have done it without my mother's assistance. And it all just began with a "yes," can you believe that?!" – Kal Holczer, Founder, Chairman Elite Excursions

Immediate Goal:

What is your attachment style in relationships based on the four discussed in the chapter: secure attachment, anxious-ambivalent, dismissive-avoidant or fearful-avoidant? How has that contributed to who you are today as a leader in your relationships (business, friendships, and love).

Can you recall one past relationship and see how it prevented/limited your success in the relationship? How does that change your perspective now?

<u>End-of-Chapter Exercise</u>

Think about a relationship that left you in a negative place and recall that time period. Whether it was a bad business partner, a relationship gone sour, write down the following: How did it affect you? What was the valuable lesson learned in that experience? Perhaps it is trusting in yourself; in having resilience in strength, discernment, and better policies in your office.

_____

_____

_____

_____

_____

_____

_____

Recommended reading:

- ○ **Resonant Leadership**, by *Annie McKee and Richard E. Boyatzis*
- ○ **Self-Compassion: Stop Beating Yourself Up and Leave Insecurity Behind**, by Kristen Neff, PhD.
- ○ **The Wisdom of Compassion**, by *The Dalai Lama*

PART 4

GROW. REVEAL.
INNOVATE. TRANSFORM.

Innovate
The *Commitment* to Change

"Innovative humans are not those who only chart progress, but change it." - Neeta Bhushan

When Richard Branson was stuck in Puerto Rico about 30 years ago he found himself unable to meet a beautiful lady friend in the British Virgin Islands because his flight was cancelled due to a lack of passengers. In that moment, he decided he was fed up with airlines not looking after its people. His high level of EmotionalGRIT gave him the idea of rounding up all the stranded passengers, hiring a plane and taking them all to BVI. In Branson's words, "I…borrowed a blackboard and as a joke wrote Virgin Airlines…$39 one way to BVI." After one phone call to Boeing, Branson had negotiated the rental of his first 747, and Virgin Airlines was born. Committed to change the aviation game, Branson fitted the back of every chair with a TV screen and was the first to introduce in-flight entertainment. Constantly asking questions such as, "What can we change to improve this experience?" are precisely what has allowed billionaire Branson to launch so many hugely successful companies across so many different sectors and markets.

Are you committed to change? Do you have the GRIT it takes to recognize an opportunity to deliver a better experience? How can you innovate and make the world a little more as you wish it to be?

CHAPTER TEN

EMOTIONAL FLEXIBILITY TO INNOVATE

"I believe you have to be willing to be misunderstood if you're going to innovate." – Jeff Bezos

Chapter Intention: I am stretching and growing, becoming my most flexible, empathetic self. I am readying my mind, body, and spirit for true innovation in my life and within my organization. The new things I am learning are changing my leadership style and narrative.

Chapter Checklist

- Too often we flex only our physical muscles, neglecting those of the spirit or mind. Accepting and adapting to failure is one way we can flex a muscle; implementing new life choices is another.
- Understanding how your emotions affect your body and overall health will help position you for taking control of your human potential.
- During the stage of **Innovate,** the key characteristics to explore are adaptability and flexibility to change.

INNOVATE

In entering the **innovate** stage of the GRIT journey, after piecing together the puzzle of **reveal,** you should now have an identity you want to claim as yours. This includes being able to let go of some of those limiting beliefs, building your emotional intelligence, and strengthening your inner will to navigate life's imperfect journey.

In your self-reflection, you may have become aware of some of the people, networks, projects, or even ideas that no longer serve you. Being able to direct your focus on how you intend to shape your thoughts and your mindset will make you the champion of your new world. Did you make a list of things that you will be doing less of? Perhaps there are certain groups of people that you have matured beyond who do not necessarily contribute to your growth, but remain in your life out of habit, loyalty, and familiarity. But are you the same person as you were three years ago? Five years ago?

Physiologically and on a cellular level, your body has gone through massive changes. Your cells are not the same as they were seven years ago, and even you are not emotionally the same as you were seven years ago. As humans, we evolve, and that is the beauty of the GRIT journey: the road to transformation and up-leveling your potential. So why would you keep a group, society, or network of friends that no longer meet your same interests or add value to enhancing your growth as an individual? This is something to keep in perspective since many leaders and executives, as they climb up the ladder of influence, are often faced with members of their community or family who haven't accepted their growth. Therefore, feelings of resentment, guilt, and hurt may arise. The common response is "you have changed," when, in fact, yes, you have evolved, and perhaps now you are on different wavelengths, which isn't a bad thing and should be appreciated. So naturally, the conversations, interests, and discussions you engage in may change, and you decide whom you want to focus your time on. You may be drawn to those who contribute to society at a higher level or play and grow in their interests in a manner similar to yours.

Acceptance of change is not an easy one. It's not easy for our team members, and it's certainly not easy for family members and friends who have seen you emerge anew. It can be the hardest thing for them to embrace—because it is simply different. It's not your responsibility to change their perspective as the responsibility is on them, yet you should appreciate and notice from a third person's perspective that the situation is the way that it is and accept the new shape of the relationship. You may realize the distance may grow even more, or that the relationship may take shape in a new way altogether—or, yes, you may end up closing that chapter of your life accordingly.

People enter your life in seasons, showing up at times you may least expect, and may serve a purpose to teach you more about what you need to learn about yourself. That is the beauty of human relationships.

We need to develop the ability to practice detachment. We embrace a relationship for however long it lasts, and the wisdom to let it go when it affects our ability to focus on life's greater plan. Hence, other doors and opportunities open we are aware of those around us.

Think about it, as our cells go through a full shift every seven years, we have the opportunity, beginning today, to innovate. Shed away the layers of what you don't want in your life, letting go of the heaviness and toxicity of negative thinking and negative people— and move towards a world of new opportunities.

Check-in

- What are you willing to do more of today?
- Have you started your Morning Bliss at least three times a week?
- Have you been able to close a chapter of your life that has been weighing on you, instead of waiting for it to magically disappear?

Workplace Innovation

Did you know that Anne Chwat, Senior VP of International Flavors and Fragrances, originally planned to be a teacher? *Forefront Magazine* featured her in an article that tells of her much different career path, leading to tremendous success at Seagram, BMG Music, and Burger King.

> "Chwat, who originally set out to be a teacher, has traveled a career path that led her to share a witness interview room with John Gotti; facilitate merger and acquisition deals in

211

the fast-paced, high-stakes Wall Street of the early 1990s; negotiate a move that transformed the music industry; and take a major fast-food chain public (and then private). While she ended up in roles she never envisioned, she has experienced a great amount of success…"

Chwat, when asked about her greatest asset to date, determined that flexibility has had the largest impact on her path and leadership. "Flexibility is extremely important. It can take you in directions you never would imagine." Chwat not only brings flexibility as a core component into her leadership team, but she enacts flexibility in her everyday life with those she mentors and manages. "I try to be flexible with the women who work for me because women often have different issues and responsibilities than men."

Leaders like Chwat are rare and powerful in their organizations. By matching vision with thoughts and thoughts to actions, Chwat has created a leadership style of transparency and flexibility in order that she can mentor individuals she serves to set up the organization for its greatest success.

Flexibility builds resiliency

If you lift weights at a gym or in your home, there are moments of fear and triumph. We don't lift weights or exercise to succeed, necessarily. We do so to become stronger and to gain the right kind of mass or muscle. This chapter is all about lifting your emotional bar and setting a new record for yourself. By learning to flex difficult emotional muscles, you are learning a trait that will stick with you forever: resiliency.

According to the Johnson & Johnson Human Performance Institute:

> "As adversity presents itself, pushing to expand your emotional capacity by training and "flexing" your "muscles" of self-control, empathy or patience during these storms,

your ability to adapt to and interpret these storms in a positive way may result in becoming more resilient in any future storms you encounter."

Resiliency isn't born out of agreeable times. Not even close! True resiliency is gained after situations of emotional turmoil or defeat, often bringing an individual to an introspective dialogue about the "why" of what has happened, enabling them to see the bigger picture to learn and adjust. Emotional resiliency is an absolute must-have for any leader, as it determines their capacity for empathy and true mentoring.

Emotions and resiliency in the workplace

Many times when I visit workplaces, I can quickly identify workplace issues that lead back to a certain style of leadership: a leader I call emotionally detached. I quickly remind and show the CEOs and leaders that I work with that a lack of emotions in the workplace leads to lower resiliency of teams and higher rates of failure. How? It happens more often than you may think. Open communication leads to a culture that allows emotions, transparency, and above all, empathy. Take away open communication between team members and their leaders and peers and you're left with individuals that harbor hurt feelings. These feelings can quickly spiral into broken communication that harms relationships, allowing distrust and toxicity to take hold of an organization. Too many pockets of negativity can lead to a poor workplace culture, which has an inherent effect on workplace success and the organization's ability to weather big changes, whether staffing, industry or otherwise.

Sometimes a disruption or change can seem too big. The emotions surrounding the vastness of a situation can greatly affect resiliency within the mind or emotions related to resiliency. This can create large amounts of anxiety and stress. We discussed in the first few chapters what a profound impact stress has on our lives and on innovation as a whole and how our brain processes fear (either fighting it or running away). To take the correct steps as leaders entrusted with big decisions, we must let emotions in to build resilience. Here's why.

Ivey Business Journal published a piece on why emotional intelligence matters in the workplace. They cited studies showing how CEOs make decisions in times of conflict or stress:

> *"Various studies show that CEO's make many decisions intuitively, mainly because they can't wait for all the facts. The studies also show that leaders' best thinking and decisions are grounded in emotional as well as intellectual intelligence. Authenticity, vulnerability and empathy are critical to success. Above all, the studies clearly demonstrate that there is a strong link between emotionally intelligent leadership and employee engagement, client satisfaction, and the bottom line. An organization that does not recognize the need to embed emotional intelligence in its culture and its leaders does so at its peril."*

The article also mentioned that to have success as a leader, an individual must have these three important qualities:

- They must articulate a vision and hold a strongly lived value system.
- Individuals must be open to creating and mentoring other leaders who make change happen.
- Leaders must exhibit resilient and emotionally intelligent leadership.

> You have the capability to correctly steer their respective ships in times of great turmoil—whether short storms, or choppy seas, because you lead with an open heart, embrace change and lean into the discomfort or surrender into knowing and trusting that the season of life shall pass.

Imperfectly Perfect

You are the architect of your life. At any point, it is your responsibility whether you are leading a household in charge of your family or as the head of a large multinational organization to continuously focus your efforts checking in with yourself. This is how your emotional awareness is strengthened. We discussed just a few chapters ago of the importance of creativity, and thought-leadership around removing perfectionism from the workplace. There is no greater killer to innovation than striving for perfectionism. As you have already learned it is simply intense fear of failure. Which cause rigidity and inflexibility in a very short amount of time. It stalls new thoughts, negates emotions and develops a culture of stagnancy.

Being emotionally aware is to be in tune with the inner chatter, the strokes of genius, and waves of inspiration inside your mind. These develop when working on a new project, creating a new business, writing a new article, or trying a new activity. This is the emotional equivalent of lifting weights.

Here are five reasons why perfection kills emotional intelligence:

1. **Decisions.** Perfection stalls important decisions, eliminates team dialogue, and causes organizations to simply "float" instead of paddle. Want to know how perfection disables decision-making? *Psychology Today* had an excellent piece on the mind of a perfectionist, showing how those that sought perfection instead of innovation stalled in decisions in these ways:

   - Perfectionists review their work repeatedly, never allowing it to move to the next step.
   - Perfectionists spend all of their time error-checking instead of gut-checking, often reading over single paragraphs two or three times.
   - Perfectionism may complicate the work/life balance, often making leaders feel they must work extra hours to "measure up."
   - Perfectionism robs teams of needed opportunities to learn and grow, creating hostility when a leader won't give up a task, allowing someone else to try.

2. **Pressure.** Perfectionism has one constant: pressure. It places enormous pressure to achieve, which ties to an individual's overall self-worth. Perfectionism limits a career path, often not allowing a leader to get to the next level.

3. **Fear.** Being deathly afraid of failing, I recognize the deep role perfection has played in my own life. The main reason why I stayed in my toxic marriage for as long as I did was because I didn't want to "fail." Failure allows us to grow and see perspectives from a different lens.

4. **Risk-averse.** This could also be called "playing it safe." When you are in control, you determine the outcomes. As we learned earlier in the book, we are never really in total control.

Uncertainty and surrendering are difficult for perfectionists due to the sheer fact that they take power away. However, recognizing this 'loss of power' can allow the most transformational and creative aspects of us to come alive.

5. **Expectations.** As human beings, we long for connection and sometimes believe we must "fill in the box" to fulfill the expectations of society. We then don't allow ourselves the opportunity to expand and celebrate our uniqueness; we fail the communities we are serving by diminishing our own light.

> Being emotionally aware is to be in tune with the inner chatter, the strokes of genius, and waves of inspiration inside your mind.

Let's work on building your emotional strength so that you can recognize and pay attention to the signals that come up, preventing you from unleashing your best innovation yet. The time is now; not for perfection, but for real, genuine, soul-quenching potential—the kind you won't find in a gym, but often while reading late at night reading and during moments of reflection.

Understanding the dilemma of being stuck

Think about when you were feeling stuck, whether in a relationship, a career you hated, or a choice that you didn't want to make. You could easily continue the same path, keeping consistency as your core focus. But there is magic just ahead. When we decide to take the other path, we experience the largest change, contributing to greater fulfillment and longer-term happiness.

Many fears arise with change. Expansion into the unknown is beneficial, and it can create wild success for companies and startups. If you are looking for success, it is absolutely a game-changer, and it is the key component to enhancing your human potential in every arena of your life. I believe that being adaptable and flexible creates a culture of innovation in every environment. Remember, the opposite of monotony and structure is flexibility and adaptability. For us to carve out new purpose, thoughts, and actions, we must create safe spaces for failure. In today's tech landscape, we live by the term "fail fast." This gives us room to shift, and pivot accordingly. The simplest shifts have been a wild contributor to advances in humanity on a variety of levels.

One of the most important elements of being on the path to revolutionary is recognizing when it's time to pivot, when it's time to wholeheartedly embrace change.

When things don't go as planned, it's a leader's job to assess the situation and take the appropriate steps. Sometimes it even means pivoting to a new relationship, process, or career. Other times it might mean a new move to a city by yourself, or an audit, where leaders dissect what went wrong.

As a leader, you must take incredible risk by leaping, almost like a toad in a pond, trusting in the muscles in your legs and the strength of mind to get you across safely. Each phase, whether success, failure (or leaping) in this life, is part of your journey. Pivoting and moving forward is simply a part of moving forward in the GRIT process—or choosing to walk down another street altogether.

GRIT perspectives on flexibility and adaptability

"The depth of what you create is mirrored by the depth of who you are. When you passionately commit to self-actualize and be radically real, you create the conditions for your most expanded creativity to shine through. In many of the startup CEOs that I work with and I've coached over the past decade learning the strength of adapting as fast as possible with the rising changes in the ever changing fast paced entrepreneurial environment offers a great container for success for the founder and is often the differentiator. With uninhibited access to your creativity, you can innovate and transform the world in ways previously unimaginable." – Justin Milano, Founder, CEO, GoodStartups

"A few years ago, one fine day I decided to help entrepreneur's pro-bono. I decided to offer my time and advice to anyone who wanted it—with no strings attached. There was absolutely no intention to make any money from these interactions, but the sheer desire to help selflessly. The more I gave, better I became as a professional. Over a period of three years, I ended up helping almost 400 entrepreneurs pro bono. None of those interactions were documented; even then it gave me lot of good Karma. These meetings translated in 4 angel investments, advisory equity from several startups, deep discounts on several products & services, and one co-founder position. So, I decided to build a platform called KarmaCircles to make it easy for any professional in the world to share "Karma" with anyone else. To me, that filled a void and changed the world." – Deepak Goel, Founder, KarmaCircles

Immediate Goal:

Take the next 10 minutes, and reflect on the strategies given in this chapter. How have you used flexibility as a characteristic in your life thus far? Name two ways (business or personal) that you can be more adaptable starting this week (with your time schedule, children, or team members)?

<u>End-of-Chapter Exercise</u>

How flexible are you?

Let's take a look at your ability to be flexible and adaptable as a leader. Can you name three instances in which being adaptable and flexible in bending your rules contributed to a better outcome in your business or personal life?

1. _____

_____

_____

2. _____

_____

_____

3. _____

_____

_____

Next, let's look at the actual result associated with the change that you made, and its effects on your life. Did your business grow by a certain percentage or did you begin a new hobby? Perhaps you let go of a project that jeopardized your health. Write it down below, for each of your answers above.

1. _____

_____

_____

2. _____

_____

_____

3. _____

_____

_____

Recommended reading:

- o *The Power of Full Engagement*, by Jim Loehr
- o *Fear, Failure, and Flexibility: in Four Classrooms*, by Robert Rose, Ph.D.
- o *Moral Tribes: Emotion, Reason, and the Gap Between Us and Them*, by Joshua Greene

CHAPTER ELEVEN

GRATITOOLS:
A TOOLBOX LOADED WITH
A NEW PERCEPTION
AND PERSPECTIVE

"The more you praise and celebrate your life, the more there is in life to celebrate." – Oprah Winfrey

Chapter Intention: I am committed to looking at life from a different perspective. I honor that outside people and influences may have their own perception—and that has no effect on me. I celebrate with gratitude the new insights that are forming.

Chapter Checklist

- Discover your new abilities to add gratitude into your daily life.
- Embrace the different perspectives and opinions of others that you cannot change.
- Understand how vulnerability in your leadership is a profound part of your transformation.

GRATITOOLS and Gratitude

This chapter is focused on providing you with tools to shape your world. Being adaptable to the seasons of adversity and triumph over the sometimes unexpected hurdles of life mentally prepares you for achieving inner strength.

It's from that place where big shifts in other areas of your life are not only achievable, yet where the most expansion of your potential lies. This is of course an ongoing practice.

> Just like your morning bliss routine, your spiritual practice and your physical fitness, your emotional check-in is profoundly important to your overall health.

One of the single most efficient ways to sustain your new identity and physically change your emotional state in minutes is the art of giving and expressing thanks. There is a joy in extending gratitude. Gratitude for where you are today, who has contributed to where you are, and the gratitude for the people around you that support you, respect, and admire you, and look up to you.

The word gratitude comes from the Latin word *gratia*, which means grace, graciousness, or gratefulness. In some ways, gratitude encompasses all of these meanings. Gratitude is a thankful appreciation for what an individual receives, whether tangible or intangible. With gratitude, people acknowledge the goodness in their lives. In the process, people usually recognize that the source of that goodness lies at least partially outside themselves. As a result, gratitude also helps people connect to something larger than themselves as individuals — whether to other people, nature, or a higher power.

Gratitude as a cure for depression?

The Greater Good Center at the University of Berkeley, CA published a study that took 48 people who were on a waiting list to receive psychotherapy and who reported problems ranging from depression and anxiety to substance abuse and eating disorders. Participants were assigned to one of three groups:

- In the first, they were asked to keep a gratitude journal. Instructing the participants to jot down a list of the things they were grateful for.
- The second group kept a journal about kindness, and write down any act of a kind gesture they were able to pay it forward to others.
- The third group, which acted as a control, was asked to write about their daily mood, expectations for the following day, their sense of connectedness with others, and their overall satisfaction with life."

The results actually demonstrated overall general response to quality of life, fulfillment and happiness, but more importantly showcased the efficacy of how in short periods of time (14 days) in this particular study, brief self-administered positive psychological strategies aren't just for happy people who are looking to be happier. They can work for a group that actually are in need of help.

> Being adaptable to the seasons of adversity and triumph over the sometimes-unexpected hurdles of life mentally prepares you for achieving inner strength.

In the distraction laden, over busy and chaotic world we are in, it is no wonder that in the last decade a surge of anxiety, depression, and overall stress related diseases have increased. Using the power of positive psychology, and creating new pathways and connections of not only understanding your emotions and changing your emotional states, but also taking the time to self-reflect on what your emotions are telling you rather than try to pacify it with distractions.

Additionally, it then falls within your responsibility to choose a different state as a result, and gratitude is a simple reminder that can easily give you feelings of joy even in the most adverse situations.

We see this in religious groups how the power of prayer, giving thanks and appreciation can dramatically shift one's mindset from mood, if experiencing feelings of sadness, anger, frustration, or essentially any negative state to one of awe and contentment.

In my own life, in all of the seasons of my life's challenges: including the tremendous loss of watching both of my parents and my brother pass on, the force of tremendous gratitude and the power of prayer and meditation were my saving grace. It gave a different meaning and perspective on life. During the grieving process, I experienced the sad feelings of anger, and the pain of losing one parent. Losing a sibling unexpectedly conditioned me into believing that the season of sadness wouldn't go away. The power of prayer didn't cure my parents' illness, but it provided a sense of visceral calmness, and a tendency to look for the silver lining, even when at times it felt like the dark tunnel was miles away from getting brighter.

> Using the power of positive psychology, and shifting your mindset in not only understanding your emotions and changing your emotional states, but also taking the time to self-reflect on what your emotions are telling you rather than try to pacify it with distractions.

It is no secret how that for centuries, philosophies around prayer, services, giving thanks, choosing benevolence, and focusing on positive emotions directly have been shown to affect your overall being, notwithstanding your physical states as well.

In an experiment conducted by the Institute of HeartMath:

> *"Some human placental DNA was placed in a container from which they could measure changes in it. Twenty-eight vials of DNA were given. Each researcher had been trained in how to generate and feel feelings, and each had strong emotions. What was discovered was that the DNA changed its shape according to the feelings of the researchers: When the researchers felt gratitude, love, and appreciation, the DNA responded by relaxing and the strands unwound. The length of the DNA became longer. When the researchers felt anger, fear,*

frustration, or stress, the DNA responded by tightening up. It became shorter and switched off many of its codes."

Similarly, another study by the institute showcased similar experiences of DNA change with water. In this study, when the water was exposed to positive association and positive emotional states like love and more importantly gratitude statements- it responded also to a relaxing and unwinding of the DNA strands. This tells us specifically, how the power of positive mindset can shift the structural changes in our DNA. Which leads into the next discussion of choosing your emotional states and utilizing GRATITOOLS as a way to catapult your daily success.

With this framework it becomes easy to then create a rippling domino effect of the energy you transmit into the world.

On being human

Of course there will be times of being deeply tested, where as a having a strong external core gives off the facade that you have it all figured out and put together. We try our hardest to hide some of the pains we may face in our own lives. As we've understood the reasons behind that in previous chapters. The key characteristic for revolutionary shifts in your thinking is allowing yourself to be open to vulnerability. The world is in need of raw honesty. Living in the shifting paradigm of today where your Facebook feed showcases the highlight reel of the most exciting aspects of your life, yet behind the veneer is a human that has different aspects, different waves of life, the turning points in your evolution—and you are not the only one. When you give permission to share, it allows for better connection deeper and meaningful relationships.

> The key characteristic for revolutionary shifts in your thinking is allowing yourself to be open to vulnerability.

Insights into how to pivot, and make better decisions, and offers an opening for others to respond in from a new perspective. On a professional level, vulnerability in embracing your humanness naturally makes you more authentic, and more authenticity allows for deeper empathy—the understanding and care from your colleagues and partners. Making you more human also enables the facilitation of trust. And trust is key in building any business sustaining the highs and the multiple inflection points in a company.

This is essentially what we are building, a society with easier access to build bridges with one another realizing that above all the path to enhance your human potential in all areas of your life is with the realization that you are not alone. Just as much as you may have your internal triggers and insecurities, the other person on the other side of the table has just about the same types of triggers. Yet, you would not even know or be attune to it because take for instance the religious divides and bigotry that causes separation and fear— because of judgment and putting someone in a "certain box" you limit and restrict any perspectives of even being open to empathy simply because of the walls you have built.

> The world is in need of raw honesty.

In leadership, the strategy for leading wars and playing a political game always started with, "don't reveal all of your cards." Vulnerability has often been taught as a sign of weakness.

Yet when you break through that mentality by creating opportunities for shared vulnerability, your businesses, companies, communities, and economies will operate with a flourishing sense of transparency and abundance. There won't be any fear of overprotecting because there is a sense of shared trust, shared understanding, and finally, empathy for humanity.

GRIT perspectives on vulnerability and shifting to a new perspective

"It means life. It means the constant evolution of a being and society. It's the truth of why we are here and what we need to do. Growing up with traditional south Asian parents living in Australia, the pressures were immense to continuously become, and sometimes it was not ever enough. Yet, in this life we are constantly called upon to grow with new experiences and challenges. And growth only has its impact if you can share the experience, learn from it and sustain a transformation. Vulnerability is always much easier thought of than exercised but practicing it builds trust, communication and openness to possibilities. These two virtues alongside truthfulness, have kept things real, allowed me to set boundaries, acknowledge failures and celebrate success. It has helped me build my tribe, which is undoubtedly important to thrive! It's about striving to practice all the letters of that acronym and know you are enough!" - Shantini Iyenger, Chief Lifestyler and Co-founder of Organica Lifestyle

"Building a law practice right out of law school in New York City was absolutely crazy. Curiosity drove me to truly understand my clients' needs and build my business model around them as well as gaining a different perspective in the direction of where I wanted to have the most impact for the clients I served. Resilience was necessary, as I had to learn by trial and error. I had to fail and pick myself up again. Authenticity mattered because it helped me differentiate my firm from others, rather than emulating what everybody else was doing, I tried to create a firm that was an authentic reflection of my values, which is what is reflected in my book and how majority of my practice is focused on social enterprise businesses incorporating both impact and monetary gain." -- Kyle Westaway, CEO Westaway Law, Author of *Profit and Passion*

Immediate Goal:

Take a few moments to reflect on completing Parts 1-4. You are ready to be Revolutionary Leaders with your newfound EmotionalGRIT.

End-of-Chapter Exercise

- Set aside a time, perhaps ten minutes in the morning or evening of every day.

- Celebrate your three wins, say them out loud, share it with a loved one. This could be a great way to begin morning meetings, or evening dinner conversations.

- How often can you create systems to express gratitude on a daily basis? Before eating a meal, when you first wake up as part of your routine, before sleeping, with those that you love? These are just some examples.

_____

_____

Think of a time that you were embarrassed or felt uncomfortable or anxious to share with a group of people that you deeply respect and admire—and write it down below.

_____

_____

_____

Look in the mirror, and recite: "I have something to tell
Look in the mirror, and recite: "I have something to tell
you that I'm not quite comfortable with."

Now, see if you can practice this with a partner and have
both of you analyze each other's body language. What
happened? Was your body posture closed or open? Are
you pacing? Where are you looking?

Describe a time in your relationship with your spouse or
significant other when you were absolutely mortified,
embarrassed, and almost lied to cover up the truth.

_____

_____

_____

How did you feel in that moment?

_____

_____

_____

What were you afraid of sharing/owning up to/admitting?

_____

_____

_____

What would have happened if you told that person?

_____

_____

_____

PART 5

GROW. REVEAL.
INNOVATE. **TRANSFORM.**

Transform
Take Responsibility and Take *Action*

"Every transformation resides in the imagination's ability to see what is not yet there or what is deep inside yearning to break free."

Got the juice it takes to truly reinvent yourself? Transform yourself?

In 2005, inspirational speaker Joe Cross weighed 310 pounds (140 kg). For 30 years, Joe tried both traditional and non-traditional medication to solve his problem to no avail, including various diets in short sprints. At that time Joe consumed processed foods daily and smoked and drank alcohol regularly. He had a feeling his eating habits were causing his poor health and believed that the medication and doctors were unable to give him the results he so desperately wanted. That same year, at age 40, doctors had told Cross that he would die early. In a display of true EmotionalGRIT, Cross took action. He decided to do a juice fast for 60 days. Though he felt groggy initially, he soon began to notice a huge change in is mood and energy levels. In only 49 days, Cross had lost a whopping 67 pounds (30kg) and almost halved his cholesterol. So radical was this transformation that Joe made it his mission to go out there and share his knowledge and the documentary of his journey to help others transform, *Fat, Sick & Nearly Dead*, in 2010 became a worldwide hit. He now is the founder and CEO of "Reboot with Joe," an organization with an aim of educating the people who are lost in bad diets, make their own transformations.

Do you have the EmotionalGRIT to take real action in your own life?

CHAPTER TWELVE

ELEVATE YOUR LIFE WITH NEW ANCHORS

"There is no passion to be found playing small, in settling for a life that is less than the one you are capable of living."
– Nelson Mandela

Chapter Intention: Now is my time. I'm equipped with everything I need for action and transformation. I'm ready to upgrade my personal, internal software.

Chapter Checklist

- Begin to build your action plan for successful implementation
- Understand how the GRIT process is continuous and ongoing roadmap
- Connect the dots of your life and what it means moving forward

TRANSFORM

It's time for transformation. It's time to channel everything that you have learned from the GRIT process into an actionable plan to prepare for the revolution in your life. From today onward, you will take deliberate ownership of how you show up in the world and how you regulate your emotional health.

You will own the best practices of ensuring that the energy you derive from your internal strength will affect the world around you.

In these last three chapters, we will focus on your game plan. Your development is an ongoing process. Use the EmotionalGRIT book as your compass to navigate the parts of the GRIT journey that need a deeper look.

In this chapter, we will recap the steps of GRIT and what you need to do in order to take action in being an emotional leader of your life.

In Chapter 13: We will summarize what this looks like in the world you are shaping around you: including your family, your friends, your businesses, your companies, and the global community. You will build from your microsphere and see how it influences your new walk into the world with your new established EmotionalGRIT.

In Chapter 14: Lastly, you will examine this question: what are your responsibilities for the future of humanity in a shifting world? What are you willing to do to create revolutionary change? What is required to help you get there? How will this shape the future landscape in cultivating the new era of human potential?

This is what you have already learned in the GRIT process:

Understanding your emotions through:

- awareness
- acceptance
- commitment
- action

Grow: a recap

Without growing you cease to exist. How we view and go about the world, based within our own nature and bodies, starts with this first step. We need to cultivate the ability to be open and expansive including our own awareness and inquisitiveness. Think about it. When you are not putting effort into yourself in expanding your thought process, your creativity, and your own evolution, how does it reveal itself into the world around you? What about when the initial honeymoon phase is gone from your newfound friendships and relationships? What are you willing to do to think differently to keep the spark and the momentum going? What tends to happen as a result? How will you now plan accordingly to chart a different direction or to make sure the seeds you are planting in cultivating and growing your relationships are sustainable and evolve into their highest potential?

Relationships, the connection, the desire, and the curiosity can slowly diminish over time.

The same holds true for any new hobby, interest, or 'passion project.' Passion really is another process of discovery and curiosity. Curiosity is one of the key characteristics of the EmotionalGRIT journey.

Extraordinary humans like you who are on the road to building exceptional emotional leadership and awareness are driven by the pursuit to know more. Without it, other distractions emerge and take hold, and then suddenly the interest is lost.

For leaders in business who are shaping cultures, continuously finding ways to break out of complacency in order to move with the ever-shifting markets, it is a continuous must to reinvent, or like a phoenix, rise again anew. When you reach a plateau in your governance, it affects on your impact and contribution in the world, and of course, your bottom line.

So what strategy is needed?

In our GROW section, we learned:

- How to commitment to see ourselves clearly, including answering three questions honestly:
- What patterns have dominated your journey so far?
- What stories have you told yourself about your past?
- How have you made your decisions in the past?

In the REVEAL section, we looked deeper, examining

- What are your current belief and value systems?
- How do you personally experience a culture of fear?

- What are your key strengths and unique abilities?
- How do the perspectives of others effect you and your communication style?
- What has been your attachment style?
- How can your curiosity and boundaries fuel your path?
- Have you fully embraced the art of forgiveness?

In our INNOVATE section, we committed to action, asking:

- What is your commitment?
- What are you willing to let go of, do more of?
- What are you becoming?
- Who are you NOW?

Now, together, we will create your plan!

> "Effort and courage are not enough without purpose and direction."
> – John F. Kennedy

The road through resilience

Adversity will always be a part of life. What sets you apart is the tenacity and fierce capacity to rise up again and again. In every single stage of your life, there will be an ebb and flow, including dark times.

It's not about avoiding them altogether; it's about understanding how to navigate through the challenging aspects of life in embracing some of its toughest pain points. Everyone will have them to some degree or another. Finding strength isn't about relishing the role of the victim; it is embracing the valuable lessons that strengthen your core as a human as a result. It is actually utilizing the silver lining in each scenario so that you can make better decisions as a result.

Your GRIT requirements:

- It is time to direct all of newly learned skills in building your new anchor points.
- Think about the roadmap you are now creating.
- Transformation requires thinking differently and coming up with your individual strategies of how this will look for your own life.
- Have you ever thought about a life roadmap of how you wish to share your gifts in the world?
- Or about taking a survey of the big areas of your life and how to respond your enhancing your overall human potential?

> Adversity will always be a part of life. What sets you apart is the tenacity and fierce capacity to rise up again and again.

Over the next few pages, you are encouraged to take time to fill out the sections and self-reflect. Change does not occur overnight; however with an actionable game plan, your journey into transformation is already beginning.

Some tips to consider while deeply diving into this personal work:

- Keep an additional journal handy and separate each section.
- Notice that in the back of the book under *References and Resources*, you have additional access to keep you organized and a "quick reference" sheet to refer back to.
- You may find that in your internal discovery, you will want to recommend this book and your newly equipped skillset with your friends, family, colleagues, and teammates, because as you GRIT you will find the urge to bring those in your world along too. (That's the next chapter)

- Properly set aside time per section. As a reference, for the GRIT leaders, it is recommended to take an hour an evening this week to reflect and come back to it as you may find there is more to write down.

The eight categories for cultivating your optimized human potential are below. Remember it begins with your emotional regulation and building your emotional endurance. In enhancing your brain potential and rewiring your internal software from years of "programming" —society's conditioning of how you should be, how you should think, worrying about what society will say or afraid of fully speaking your truth. You are now past that as leaders.

> "*The biggest challenge to self-control is emotional regulation. Successful people know how to make their emotions their servants rather than their masters.*"- Paul TP Wong

Emotional States

As you have learned, your emotions are the key drivers to your behavior dynamics with others—but it begins with you. Please list below: how are you looking to better understand your negative emotional states and replace them with the positive emotional states?

From the lists of positive and negative states in the Reference section at the back of the book:

1. Which are you committed to experiencing daily? (Happy, grateful, playful etc.)

Identify your top two here:

_____

_____

_____

Which of those are in need of a massive overhaul? (Angry, worried, stressed etc.)

_____

_____

_____

2. Character assessment:

Out of the ten characteristics of GRIT, which of them are you ready to embody more of?

_____

_____

_____

Why are these characteristics important to you?

_____

_____

_____

How will this enhance the leadership in your life?

_____

_____

_____

3. Personal EmotionalGRIT Kit:

During periods of entering a low emotional state, stressful periods in the day are part of everyday balance. Stress management is a mandatory part of the shifting world that we are living in today. You are in control. You have all of the tools including the newfound awareness to choose better decisions as a result every single day. How you decide to show up everyday. How you will take the necessary steps to ensure your emotional strength and wellbeing through the course of your new path forward. This is you nourishing and feeding your emotional fitness. So what are you putting in it so you can replenish it immediately as you feel your emotional reservoir beginning to tank? Here are some examples for you to get started. Remember: Emotion = Energy in motion

- **Movement**: Even 60 seconds of movement throughout the day will add bursts of energy and contribute to increasing your productivity, awareness, and of course, your fitness. So take a few moments to note: What you are committing to here? (Dancing, yoga poses, pushups, running, jumping jacks, rebounding on a trampoline etc.)

- **Music**: What playlists will you be creating? What three songs first come to mind to elevate your mood? List them here?

- **Scent**: Candles, incense, essential oils. In any stressful state these are great hacks to keep at your desk, bedside, in your purse (oils), or your office. What scents make you feel calm? What rejuvenates you? What energizes and what makes you feel comforted?

- **Meditation**: Silence, quiet time, and visual meditation are ways to instantly quiet your mind. They take you into an alpha brain state. How many minutes will you be able to commit to in your EmotionalGRIT kit? Three minutes, five minutes, 20 minutes? How many times a day? Only during periods of low emotional states?

- **Journaling**: Communicating your feelings on paper, extending gratitude for your day and what you are committed to are just some examples to release, and the reasoning behind your feelings. Here's an example: "I'm feeling anxious around this opportunity?" Why: "I still believe I have Imposter syndrome and think I may not be a fit for the position."

- **Positive/inspirational podcasts, books, sacred texts, quotes**: Which ones are you focused on keeping handy? Go ahead and make a list on your phone, journal, or an email and save it in a folder called EmotionalGRIT KIT: Positive. Make a list of ten quotes that move you. You can also select one and keep it on the back of your desktop, Pinterest board, or on the background screen of your phone.

- **Funny clips, shows, videos**: Humor is the best way out of an emotionally charged state. Make a list of at least five of your favorite YouTube videos, podcasts, t.v. shows, or comedians to call on in this category. (For example: *Ellen*, *The Tonight Show with Jimmy Fallon*, *Seinfeld*)

4. Health vision:

Consider your brain and your body. What are you putting into your body? This is the only vessel you have for the rest of your life. How will you take care of this vessel? What does your food routine look like? Do you overeat? Or do you not eat during low emotional states?

Start out with the simple tasks: How much more water can you consume daily? Are you drinking enough? We know that when we are dehydrated we are less likely to make proper decisions, and are more likely to eat foods (sugar, soda, fried foods, comfort foods) to "satisfy" you temporarily that will cause an immediate crash. This process isn't sustainable and won't keep your body in the highest state possible.

What is your current nutritional state? How many superfoods can you incorporate more of?

_____

_____

_____

What are you starting your day with? Are you skipping breakfast? Do you fast before lunch? What type of lifestyle are you committed to? Pick out one option and begin out with a 30-day challenge beginning today. For example, perhaps starting with intentional eating of a green juice or smoothie with good fats and low sugar is much more powerful than orange juice, coffee and toast. Filling your vessel appropriately will also set the stage for others around you.

_____

_____

_____

Do you need additional support such as a trainer or nutritionist?

_____

5. Quality of life:

Intentionally schedule periods of fun. When was the last time you took a vacation? Or a solo trip with no phones, no devices, no distractions. For the next 30 days, how can you add more fun, different experiences, and new interests to explore in your life? (For example, planning a date night with your significant other, finally signing up for ballroom dance lessons, going for swimming lessons, or planning a day to the spa.)

Write down three things here that you will commit to now.

_____

_____

_____

6. Social and business relationships: Are the relationships in your life right now supporting you?

Make a list of the top ten people who you spend the most time with now.

_____

_____

_____

_____

_____

Make a list of five people that you would _like_ to spend _more_ time with. (Maybe you don't even know them, but they are an example of the type of group, community that you would like to know).

_____

_____

_____

_____

Now, make a list of five people who challenge you? We all need an accountability group, a sort of "board" that will help us upgrade not only our capabilities, but our future human potential.

_____

_____

_____

How will you create opportunities to meet with these people? Set up a monthly gathering or Google hangout (even if it's 30 minutes). Perhaps it's a network or a community that meets a few times a year that you can easily work into your schedule?

_____

_____

_____

Is there anyone on the list of those who you spend time with that you should be spending *less* time with? Are they not contributing to your overall growth; are they are energy suckers and not healthy to be around? Make a list below. How will your life look like and be like if you are no longer in communication with them?

_____

_____

_____

_____

> Transformation requires action. Action is committing to make it happen no matter what.

7. **Family and love life**: Based on your attachment level is how you respond in relationships.

- Questions to consider in creating your strategy for transformation:
- Are you committed to enhancing the lives of the people around you?
- Do you spend time with your children? If so, how often?
- How are your boundaries with your family life?
- Do you need to have difficult conversations in establishing your boundaries?
- How often are you spending meaningful time with your significant other?

If you are single, and only interested in short-term relationships what is the reason? What will you focus on so that you can be ready and open to the right relationships? What action steps will you take (for example, a dating service, a better online profile, a survey of the people around you that you may not have been interested in, etc.).

The quality of our emotional health and wellness significantly revolves around this piece. Being able to thrive in your personal life will make you revolutionary for the impact you wish to create in the world.

_____

_____

_____

_____

_____

_____

_____

_____

_____

8. **Additional support**:

In all of these areas, the big road to keeping up with ongoing change during phases of transformation is the support you need to keep you consistent with your new goals and objectives.

What experts, consultants, coaches, conferences, seminars, books, guides that you are willing to invest in yourself to take you to the next level of your GRIT?

_____

_____

_____

For example, the greatest athletes surround themselves with the appropriate support and work with the trainers to make sure their progress is charted. The same goes with those desiring better relationships or acquiring a new skill set.

_____

_____

_____

_____

Immediate Goal:

Remember, every person is different. Your responsibility is to implement and strategize the opportunities to enhance *your* human potential so that you can be better leaders of the communities that you serve.

_____

_____

_____

_____

GRIT perspectives on transformation

"Authenticity (congruency) is hands down, the most important attribute that has gotten me this far in my life thus far...but, this wasn't always the case! During my college experience, as I was nearing the end of my junior year, I had the opportunity to apply for the Vanderbilt Accelerator Program, which was a summer business program comprising of 16 hour days over the span of 30 days while undergraduates work closely with 6 very successful companies. This was an opportunity that I definitely wanted to take full advantage of. From the beginning—sure, I had my limiting beliefs, but I still figured I was a "shoe-in" because one of the directors of the program was one of my business professors and we got along very well! My interview was set for a weekday. So, off I went, very prepared and well dressed. During our interview and conversation, I could see that

my professor, Michael wasn't digesting my answers as well as I thought they would go down. In fact, I remember him saying these words to me: "Alex, without a doubt, you have so many unique qualities—and, at this time, you are reflecting what you think others expect of you. I'm not going to admit you into this program because I want you to go out and find your voice." Of course, this was a massive let down at the time. But as I continued on my path, with respect and further understanding of what Michael was trying to get me to understand, the more gratitude I received for my 'rejection.' The reason I am bringing up this story is because that one interview changed my life. I was urged to go out and find my voice...to create it, instead of only saying the things that I thought other people expected of me. This one lesson set me on a path of authenticity and taking full responsibility for my life. What I share in my business and life is a direct reflection to some of the biggest lessons I've learned from Michael. Congruency, consistency and value are key if you want to be very successful. When I was about 16 years old, my father took my sister and I to his job's "Bring Your Family to Work Day." That day, when my father was introducing my sister and I to a few of us co-workers, an older Asian introduced himself and told my sister that she was a beautiful young lady and then turned to me and said, "oh, sumo wrestler, huh!?" To say that I instantly became very saddened would be an understatement. So, later that day I shared with my mother what the man had said and for the first time in my life as an obese kid, she said..."well baby, if you're tired of others talking about you or making fun of you, then it's time to do something about it." Of course, this wasn't what I wanted to hear that time, but the truth is: it's what I really needed to hear then.

And for the subsequent weeks after, I gave it a lot of thought which started to direct my new actions and habits. Fast forward less than 9 months later and I had lost almost half my initial body weight. I was a brand new Alex...even to the point that people didn't even recognize me anymore." – Alex Echols, Bestselling author of *The Two Week Notice*, Founder of Ultimate Business Builders/Producer

"*This question haunts almost all entrepreneurs who started small and reached a level set by them for them. For me GRIT means constant hustling. I grew as a person when under heavy circumstances I had to work full time from the age of 17. It really made me grow and come out of all those silly and petty things that we all do in our teens. It would be unfair to say that I have revealed myself completely. To be frank I myself don't know how much more I can surprise myself at different levels of life. But one instance where I feel I revealed myself was when I was handed over a loss making company at the age of 18 and had to bear the pressure to make it running so as to provide for my family. Innovation is something that has to be and must be in a continuous loop if one has to grow and I feel me coming up with new business ventures.*

Later, I realized being a businessmen and being an entrepreneur are two distinct roles from one another. In my case, when it was experiencing intense betrayal of my own family member and was cheated upon and my company was taken over by my family member was a turning point where I learned how to trust people but with caution, and gravely tested my resilience, and even my own worth. I've realized that in business and in life the decisions that you make lead you down different roads, it's okay not to hold grudges or worry about what should you have done differently, rather it's in the forgiveness of yourself and allowing you to make better defined decisions as your rise out of the sometimes dark seasons of life." – Munnish Chadha, Global Serial Entrepreneur, Investor

"*Twelve years ago I went through a life-changing body transformation (weight loss), and five years ago I went through a* divorce. I'm from a prominent Indian family from Bangkok, Thailand. It was a tremendous shock, shame, and guilt—which tested my core strength of what society can be. While the first instance taught me that being driven yield results, the second helped me develop a sense of compassion towards myself and others especially amidst vulnerability.

Vulnerability is a true test of the human spirit, because the fear of being judged can sometimes paralyze your soul, but you realize the larger picture is that there are others who have been terrified of the 'taboo' and 'shame' around divorce, which I was allowing my story to give them strength. So, I realize that goals can be achieved through hard work and determination (and perhaps a little luck!) but not without believing in yourself (self-compassion) and having support from others. This also means supporting them in return in their time of need (compassion towards others).

I abide by these traits in both personal and professional life. I'm now in the happiest relationship in my life, married to my best friend, which has opened doors in my new walk with motherhood, establishing business in a different country, as well as expanding my love of health & wellness. This can only flourish with the right amount of support, and you are all deserving of happy & loving relationships." – Serina Bajaj, Mother, Blogger, Founder of Raisin' The Roof, Malaysia

Additional Notes:

_____

_____

_____

_____

_____

CHAPTER THIRTEEN

LEADERS: GET READY TO CHANGE YOUR WORLD

"Good judgment comes from experience and experience comes from bad judgments." – Dr. Wayne W. Dyer

Chapter intention:
To embrace a kinder lifestyle and re-think the consequences of not just our actions, but our mission.

Chapter Checklist:

- What acts of kindness can you incorporate on a daily basis?
- Would you compliment a random person in the grocery store? Or share a note of gratitude to your team member? Would you pay for the coffee for the person standing in a line behind you?
- How can you contribute to a more humanistic world?
- What is your larger purpose as a leader?

Our service to others is the hallmark of the human spirit. You are now equipped to transform the lives that you lead. While this chapter may be focused on leaders, professionals and executives; it is also a great call to action for everyone to take a closer look at how your new found GRIT will take an affect in the lives that you interact with on a daily basis. Here, we will explore how each one of you has a greater mission and a larger purpose: share your unique gifts and adding value in your world. In the chapters leading up to this, it has all been about how to fill your cup and get your emotional leadership in action, so that you can contribute to the revolutionary thinking required to uplift humanity. Because every single person when more aware, collectively can make profound shifts in being better humans for our future generations. What kind of world would that look like?

> Our service to others is the hallmark of the human spirit.

We are already learning that simple acts of kindness spread more connection, collaboration, and a more humanistic world.

Gina Otto, #1 bestselling author, has been doing this in over a decade, spreading benevolence through teaching children from around the world to pay kind acts forward. "The light in me sees the light in you, so go and spread your light," she says in her book, *Cassandra's Angels*.

Her passion has led her in deep advocacy in creating a global movement called *Change My World Now*, which focuses on building a world full of empathetic future leaders beginning teaching the importance of empathy.

Jack Ma, CEO of Alibaba.com and philanthropist, whose IPO set the record for the largest stock offering in history, says the keys to future leadership is gender inclusion. He attributes most of the success of the company to the 'secret sauce' of having more women in leadership roles. Women "hold 34% of his company's leadership roles, which is much higher than Silicon Valley tech companies." His commitment has extended to hosting Alibaba's first Global Conference on Women and Entrepreneurship in Hangzhou to promote his mission. Representing a country that historically been very, very male-dominated makes Jack Ma's humanitarian step in taking China and more important, taking a direction of new leadership with gender equality at the forefront of its mission.

The highly regarded Ashoka Changemakers platform for building leaders in creating sustainable solutions globally that will enhance traditional industries using technology and mission driven humans has begun a new campaign. By creating a free online learning platform that makes teaching empathy to school children, fun easy, and getting them prepared for effectively creating impact. Their empathy initiatives have coined it as the most important skill in the history of the universe.

CEO Bill Drayton's life mission:

> "If you aren't given the tools of applied empathy as a young child, we shouldn't be blaming you – we should be blaming us. We have to have a revolution so that all young people grasp empathy and practice it. This is the most fundamental revolution that we have to get through." – Bill Drayton, Founder and CEO, Ashoka

The Ashoka schools and philosophy are empowering future leaders and starting from the ground up paving the way a new paradigm of building thought leaders from a core aspect to spread empathy for direct impact with tomorrow's future.

What does this mean for your company, business or organization?

What is it going to take for GRIT to occur in your world? How will the decisions that you make going forward consciously affect the lives that you lead?

What is your ideal vision for the life you are looking to build? As revolutionary pioneers, moving the needle so that the people in your world can shape their own lives with GRIT perspectives as part of empathy based leadership. What does that signify?

With your company, what small shift can you make in the ethos of your company to spark a different conversation? How can you invite more collaboration, more creative thinking, better compassion and more empathy in and enhancing the fulfillment of the lives in your direct line of impact?

Creative mornings is an organization that emerged out of a purpose for creative community people to come together one Friday a month to engage in conversations, support, networking. Basically a free and inspiring event to allow for creative thinking. CEO Tina Roth Eisenberg, founded this free community out of her own desire to create space of genuine innovation and collaboration. It is now in 148 cities around the world, where it features hometown heroes, speakers, and talented and local artisans looking for an eclectic way to connect with others and hear their stories. This simple idea was generated from a desire for creativity and human connection, a way to congregate in meaningful ways.

Creative Talk

Is there a way for you to organize a creative mornings gathering in your community, your business, or your network? If you could focus on spreading the wildfire of intentional good, on a global scale, through one simple act, what would that act be? Creating a dent in your own microsphere doesn't have to be grandiose. Yet it could have a massive impact, through the ripple effect of altruism you are providing through purpose and empathy for others and the world.

> "Dream big and your problems become small."
> - Vishen Lakhiani

When actor and producer Rainn Wilson wanted to find a way to see more positive content on the Internet, so that videos could go viral in an inspiring and meaningful way for young people, the first thought that came to mind was engaging them at a level where the barrier to entry is low. Essentially, he created a platform for funny, short clip parodies, and sharable videos that would inspire thinking, make people laugh, but also offer a solution for positivity to be spread around the world. In 2015, his brainchild, SoulPancake, was mentioned in *Fast Company* as one of the top 10 innovative companies.

Their notable tagline is "we make stuff that matters". For the first time, thousands of users could enter an online community to participate in conversations that made them feel safe to explore "what it is to be human, issues of philosophy, spirituality, and creativity."

This solution seeker's company is now named one of the fastest growing companies in the United States.

So, there is a definite shift happening. The world is encountering a revolutionary shift in how we envision being human. We are sharing a collective set of values in realizing that we all have shared challenges. Everyone's individual journey is unique, yet the pain points and inflection points along that path are similar. It's when you are aware, and understand how that relates to a common thread, that you will walk on a path toward being a better person than you were the day before. Progress is growth. Small steps in the right direction are better than none at all.

> So now, the question for you leaders is how can you begin to make a small shift in your world?

How can you evaluate the ethos of your company, or guide your business to be a pioneer in truly thinking differently? Will you commit to additional time to provide an outlet for an "innovative, fun work day" or meaningful discussions at lunch?

How often will you volunteer, be of service, or mentor the juniors in your community? How will you create a purpose-driven center, or support a culture of curiosity, promoting budding entrepreneurs, or investing in causes that you believe will impact the lives of many? In being concerned about growth, the biggest and most innovative companies thrive on being able to create happy, inspiring, and creative work environments.

> The world is encountering a revolutionary shift in how we envision being human. We are sharing a collective set of values in realizing that we all have shared challenges. Everyone's individual journey is unique, yet the pain points and inflection points along that path are similar.

Vishen Lakhiani & Ajit Nawalkha, co-founders of Mindvalley in Kuala Lumpur, Malaysia have demonstrated just that in their company that began out of one small room. The goal was to create an online educational personal development company that would bring together bright millennials from countries around the world to Malaysia. Out of seven employees, it has grown into an international company showcasing a workforce from over 40 different countries, where 55% of their workforce is female. They have created a thriving company, with a mission-driven culture that attracts brilliant young minds and have been rated as one of the world's coolest places to work. The eclectic café style, open-area playground setting creates the perfect atmosphere for engineering a lively team dynamic.

A few years ago, CEO Andrew Hewitt thought of a way to bring together companies on the forefront of creating a mission-centered ethos attached to their tagline. As leaders, when you are more aware through GRIT, it is only natural that you will not only build businesses that are purpose-driven, but you will also collectively build a movement together. With GameChangers 500, he has been able to do just that. The company awards badges to for benefit purpose-driven companies and social enterprises on a rating system, highlighting their social commitment stance through different metrics: from their commitment to sustainability, to their capacity at reducing carbon footprints, to their mission to create a society of good. Singularity University Chief Strategy Officer Gabriel Baldinucci describes how companies can create sustainable business models that have a tremendous social benefit at their core. Gone are the days where companies need to separate these two goals. Their overarching purpose is to utilize Michael Porter's shared value theory:

This describes how "the competitiveness of a company and the health of the communities around it are mutually dependent," according to *Harvard Business Review*. In order for "these connections between societal and economic progress" to have real power, we'll have to shift our economies and redefine the future of capitalism. More specifically, the shared value model promotes ways for companies to shift economies by placing an emphasis on benefiting society at large though development, enhancement, and a mission-driven core at its center. The social responsibility allows for a different type of framework to shift the way traditional companies operate. Merging the for-profit and non-profit model- into a for benefit result.

This is what can happen when businesses practice more emotional leadership—it benefits humanity in a way that solves the world's greatest challenges. In order to do that, as Gabriel suggests, pick a mission and create a business model to stand behind the mission.

> This is creating a new landscape for the future of human potential.

Immediate Goal:

How will you immediately have an impact on the lives you touch every day? How can incorporating these essential aspects of your new leadership vision into your business life and your world make big changes as a result?

_____

_____

End-of-Chapter Exercise

Picture the ideal company culture, where your life would have purpose and meaning every day. What would that look like for you?

_____

_____

Now, imagine how that company could change the world. What would its biggest impact be?

_____

_____

How can you start that company today? What would you call it? Would it a hobby, a project, a different aspect of your current business?

_____

_____

CHAPTER FOURTEEN

HACKING YOUR REVOLUTIONARY HUMAN POTENTIAL

"If we did all the things we are capable of we would astound ourselves." - Thomas Edison

Chapter Intention: To build a company, and lifestyle, that will transform your life from top to bottom. To discover a brand that will change the world around you at the same time.

Chapter Check List:

- What is the bigger picture of your EmotionalGRIT plan?
- How will we create a revolution in your lifestyle?
- How will that revolution ripple beyond your own microsphere?

You have arrived. This requires your leadership. This is your call to action, how you will embrace your responsibility with a higher purpose. This is how you will start an inner revolution that begins to spill over in every aspect of your life. As you have become more familiar with your GRIT journey, and you understand the fundamental building blocks of empathy-based solutions for a new standard in cultivating emotional leadership- this is where you will lay out your plan. You will create a leadership style that not only shapes your own microsphere, but also enhances the quality of the lives around you, elevating your business and collectively building a better humanity. This may sound overly ambitious, but this this new era of leadership requires revolutionary potential and commitment.

The process to EmotionalGRIT—**Grow, Reveal, Innovate and Transform**—is just the beginning of the requirements you as a leader need in order to ensure the legacy and higher mission you seek in the world. By understanding your own stories and finding the wisdom in your adversities, you are now ready to chart the new frontier. You are boundless and ready, and that requires the work that only a few are willing to do. You will be one of a select group of pioneers in this next phase of leadership.

> You will start an inner revolution that begins to spill over in every aspect of your life.

For every company or client, the process of becoming revolutionary requires bravado, gusto, and commitment. Here are the key principles that this next phase of revolutionary change requires.

Revolutionary Vision

Have you established this for your personal and business life? As leaders in business, we often think of doing things cheaper, faster, and in a more innovative fashion. "Hacking" our time means being more efficient or even cutting corners, with the aim of providing more time, less stress, and more energy. But does it? What does your vision look like? It's time to assess whether the vision you are creating is truly shifting the world around you. Are you able to create the ripple effect that you desire? What is it that you are hoping to achieve in the next three to five years?

> The process of becoming revolutionary requires bravado, gusto, and commitment.

Revolutionary Scale

In upgrading your life leadership, your vision may be centered around buying a bigger house, increasing your wealth, doubling your team, or widening your network and social friendships. But the vision behind all transformational inventions of our time never started with a personal motive. Edison wasn't thinking about a summer home or his pension when he invented the light bulb.

Electricity was already flowing on city streets at the time of his breakthrough. He simply had a vision of making it affordable, so that light could flow into every home at an affordable rate. So he tasked his laboratory to find a solution. After testing 6,000 materials, they found the answer; the carbonized bamboo-based bulb revolutionized lighting the modern home.

PayPal CEO Elon Musk's was already a multimillionaire when he had a crazy vision to create a colony on Mars, a planet 140 million miles from the Earth that takes at least a month to travel to, simply because he wanted to pioneer new territory. Artificial intelligence was first imagined in the time of Constantinople. The car was invented when people were still being carted around in horse-driven carriages. Now, it's up to you to think differently. What is the real impact of a bigger house? What will truly change the quality of how you live is creating a revolutionary shift in thinking for the community you are directly impacting or hoping to affect?

Revolutionary Capabilities

Before you create your revolutionary vision, you need to enhance who you are right now. You have the right tools: the GRIT process and a system to implement every single day of your life. Think in terms of what methods and different styles of thinking you should welcome in trouble-shooting your own life. Evaluate how you can become a better human in terms of being a parent, friend, lover— and becoming an extraordinary leader in your business. What optimal energy and fitness levels would promote your highest capabilities? What are you willing and ready to commit to? What skill sets, investments, education, opportunities, advancements, and training do you need to add to achieve this?

> Think in terms of what methods and different styles of thinking you should welcome in trouble-shooting your own life.

Revolutionary Thinking

In order to open your mind to revolutionary thinking, it's good to first assess your approach to problem solving. What new thought processes are you willing to open your mind to? In science, researchers often refer to two different mindsets—vertical and horizontal thinking—which can be a useful tool to help evaluate your thinking.

Vertical thinking is an analytical and sequential process widely adopted by researchers in academia because it requires research and facts to solve a problem faster. In this method, essentially you "go deeper" in covering all of your established bases to find concrete solutions to the problem you are solving. Horizontal or lateral thinking is a broader, more creative way of thinking. It doesn't employ an investigative technique. It's more of an innovative, thinking out-of-the-box method, with a great deal of creativity. Vertical thinkers look to solve a problem and master it completely; horizontal thinkers are deeply interested in why a certain problem happens in the first place and develop a zone of expertise.

Most of us are stuck too firmly in one of these styles. How can you make your thinking shift in a horizontal or vertical direction? Before you take our bigger message out into the world, consider how you can shift your thinking in a broader way.

Other thought processes for you to consider:

- **Storytelling:** Do you deliver information in a way that lights people up and galvanizes them to your message?
- **Creative thinking**: How often do you make the time to think outside the box? How often do you sit in reflection, or take time out of each week or month to reassess, understand, and regroup your own thought processes to enhance your skills?
- **Relational thinking**: This entails the understanding the perspective and the framework of others. This is fully implementing our GRIT in empathy and human behavior

274

dynamics. How often do you take the time to understand the actions behind their behaviors?

- **Emotional toolkit and Nutritional/Physical toolkit**: In the technology world, we are constantly updating our apps, deleting the old versions to update the software on our devices. How will you update your internal software for life? What is part of your morning daily bliss and emotional toolkit from the physical and nutritional aspects that will give you premium enhancement in your life?

QUICK REVOLUTIONARY CHECKLIST

To jumpstart the revolution within yourself, here are some questions to get you going:

-- You have a brand new body every seven years and brand new bone cell regeneration every three years. How will you enhance your mission and vision within this rebirth? To increase your human potential, what will you remove? List some here:

_____

_____

-- You know that mismanaged energy can cause disease and stagnation. How will you move your body more?

_____

_____

--How will you increase your nutritional and health aspects to make you a better leader of your own life?

_____

_____

Revolutionary Interpersonal Skills

How do you influence and motivate people around you? As a leader in your home, your life, your business, and your community, how you engage in human behavior dynamics is vitally important. You have developed the tools and skillset for yourself. How do you become an even more effective communicator? What have you noticed that you need more of?

Is it compassion, adaptability, or empathy? By now, you should be closer to knowing what your gifts are.

To properly channel these traits, it takes:

- **Extraordinary Communication**: The efficiency in your delivery,
  negotiation, motivation, and momentum.
- **Extraordinary Navigation**: how you approach roadblocks, hurdles, and life.

The most impactful way you can influence and elevate your existence in business, life and love is through having extraordinary relationships. Interpersonal skills comprise a skillset required you can build with the GRIT process. Now, it's your responsibility to decide how you will continue the journey from here.

Revolutionary Purpose

What legacy do you intend on building for your future? How does your personal history inform your impact in the world? How are you committed to change your world as a result of this process? Mastering your emotions and your ongoing commitment and action required is part of the doing process. What organizations are you going to be part of? What communities and new friendships will you focus on cultivating? Who will you surround yourself with in order to enhance your future legacy?

<u>End-of-Chapter Exercise</u>

- Write a letter to your future self. Consider who you will be five years from now. What is your ideal vision of the revolution you are committed to creating for your new world?

- What action steps will you be taking toward that goal? Who are you willing to become in order to get to that point?

  _____

  _____

  _____

  _____

  _____

- Self-reflection is the most compassionate gift you can give to yourself. Please spend a designated amount of time thoughtfully planning out who you need to carry out the vision of your human potential.

  _____

  _____

  _____

  _____

  _____

Finding out how to be your best self in every capacity and discovering the fundamental necessities will give you a proper ideal and framework. Now, for the overachievers and overdoers, this is a guide. Granted you may not be able to tackle them all, yet with progress, strategy, accountability, and EmotionalGRIT as your guide, plus resources and additional materials to help keep you on track, you are on your way to long-term sustainability. The good news: you can always go back and check in with this chapter.

> Your Emotional GRIT journey is just the beginning. You are the pioneers of a new frontier you are creating.

Remember: Emotional GRIT is a way to ensure you are able to continuously rise and create a better humanity, redefining the cultural landscape of what you are in search for. In your steady work through this process, you have claimed the leadership of your future.

Acknowledgements

Thanking:

My family, my Bua, uncle Glenn and aunts for always genuinely being by my side, for lifting me up always. To my mama Chita, your strength and wisdom has always been there and the reason why I am who I am today.

To my brother Vinay, your patience and unconditional love and keen always I look up to and I cherish our walk in this life together.

To my incredible global team: Kate-Madonna, Angela, Justine, Lauren, Tariq, Dory, Alexey, Lisa, Krysta and Magda who I couldn't do this without your guidance and love. Especially, Ally, Carl, Michelle, and Johnna for your creative masterpiece in tying it all together beautifully. To my K&A creatives team, I told you once you would take on this project it would change your world immensely. It's been great seeing your growth in the process with your brilliant minds & work.

My amazing family in Asia: my extended family in the Philippines and in Delhi for being such supporters in the vision, especially Munish, Preeti, Chandni & Aman. For my tribe & awesome family in KL, Malaysia, Mindvalley family: you infused, housed, and saw firsthand changes and beautiful unfolding of this work, I totally thank and honor each of you! For my community in Singapore, Bali and the Innov8 team in Delhi I'm so incredibly blessed for your amazing and steadfast love during my creative time in writing, hosting me and making sure I was in creative flow.

For my beautiful advisors, and the shoulders you have offered when I was running in circles, Ally, Mike, Andrew, Sanjiv (V2), Jonathan, Rupal, Marquise, Jacques-Philippe, and Michaela so much appreciation and thanks for holding down the fort when needed.

To my one of a kind coach, Ajit, I love and thank you for keeping my vision in full track when it seemed otherwise never-ending.

To my dharma circle, Jess & Gina and Yasmine- I love you ladies. Harbeen & Vinay for your intense guidance and unwavering belief in me.

Yale Center of Emotional intelligence, Singularity University, Ashoka Changemakers, Women Economic Forum, Stanford Center for Compassion, and Duckworth Character labs, thank you for being pioneers in this conversation in building extraordinary leaders.

Angela, thank you for being extraordinary in your vision and deep work on GRIT in schools, the workplace and community.

To the leaders, corporations, and companies that I've interviewed, spent time with to truly understand and merge the dialogue to enhance the importance of the conversation globally across 45 countries, I celebrate you for propelling this new dialogue.

PERSONALIZE YOUR EmotionalGRIT KIT

This is a great reference to create and personalize your own EmotionalGRIT KIT for yourself, your family, teammates, and office.

This is your Toolkit to elevate your emotional states during times of stress, moments of anxiety, or to simply boost your energy throughout the day.

Here's some examples to get you thinking. Please visit EmotionalGRIT.com for additional resources and hacks to elevate your mood into peak states for more energy, efficiency, and productivity.

MUSIC

- Upbeat playlist.
- Classical, binaural beasts, brainwave noise to elevate yourself and your efficiency.

NUTRITION

- Drink water!
- Consume superfoods like cinnamon, turmeric, chaga, spirulina, chia seeds, coconut oil, flaxseeds, ashwaganda, astragaulus, cocoa, etc.

SCENTS

Incense, candles, essential oils (breathe some of your favorite scents).

MOVEMENT

- Emotion-> energy in motion.
- Move your body! Set a timer every hour to do 10 jumping jacks, 10 high kicks, 10 squats, and 10 pushups.

BREATHWORK

Deep breathing 3x in your belly to activate your parasympathetic system .

POSITIVE BOOKS /IAM STATEMENTS/QUOTES

List some of your favorites. Where can you post them? Desktop, phone, create a document for easy reach?

PODCASTS/MOVIES /FUNNY CLIPS

Humor, entertaining, enlightening, these can shift your mood in an instant.

MINDFULNESS /MEDITATION

All you need to start with is 2-3 mins. Silence. Easy breathing.

HUMAN INTERACTION

Who lights you up, who can you think about that puts a smile on your face? Who can you spend some time with or call? List them!

YOU ARE ENHANCING YOUR HUMAN POTENTIAL.

Resources

Positive Emotional states

- compassionate
- creative
- connected
- successful
- appreciated
- deserving
- loving
- playful
- calm
- excited
- thoughtful
- happy
- joyous
- kind
- content
- motivated
- peaceful
- supported
- valued
- inspired
- purposeful
- Enthusiastic
- invigorated
- friendly
- driven
- empowered
- confident
- attractive
- abundant
- limitless
- present
- fulfilled
- Relaxed

Negative emotional state

- anxious
- sad
- empty
- alone
- numb
- insecure
- unconfident
- self-critical
- misunderstood
- incompetent
- isolated
- unsupported
- outcast
- hopeless
- unloved
- worrisome
- unattractive
- stressed
- resentful
- depressed
- jaded
- bored
- inadequate
- inferior
- frustrated
- confused
- angry
- overwhelmed
- negative
- unhappy
- outdated
- old
- envious
- judged

Recap: Key Characteristics of EmotionalGRIT

GROW, REVEAL, INNOVATE, & TRANSFORM

➢ **Authenticity**: The ability to fully be yourself no matter what. Expressing the truest form of you, the quirks that make you unique, the strengths of your personality. The shortcomings that you discover about yourself and you accept anyway. It is the version of yourself that encompasses all of the things that you love without any reverence for society, family, friends, or external noise of who you are expected to be.

➢ **Drive**: If you are going to create lasting value in the world, there is definitely going to be high points and low points. The real question and emotion to consider is your tenacity and motivation for perseverance. It is easy to "give up" and quit when it seems like the universe is crashing down on you. It becomes your responsibility to adapt to the complexities and rise above with determination.

➢ **Enthusiasm:** Attitude is everything. Think of when you are having a challenging day. Everything just seems to be going the absolute worst. Car broke down, you are running late, you may haven't had anything to eat all day and you are "hangry". When you are commanding a team, your family, your friends it becomes your responsibility to change the energy in the room—even when you may be feeling your absolute worst. Operating from this emotion is a sure fire way to gain the acceptance and switch the current state of where you are at- no matter what- in an absolute instance.

➢ **Courage**: The willingness and boldness to speak, be, and share your voice, your opinion. To truly take a stance, without the consequence of hurting feelings of others, fully protecting yourself and allowing the bravado to be seen and heard unapologetically.

➢ **Curiosity**: Leading your life with this characteristic will change your business, personal relationships, love relationships and overall help further a more connected world. There is no judgment in curiosity. This is a deep understanding and inquisition to know more. To understand why, and to pursue the unknown, gain a different perspective, a different thought process, encourage openness and expansion. This is the top characteristic when surveying over 500 top leaders, executives, futurists, and thinkers.

➢ **Presence/focus:** Mindfulness, calm, awareness, peace in the busyness of the lives we currently live in is important to your internal framework. Your internal foundation, and dialogue of peace. Operating from this lens not concerned with the past nor the future, yet living in each moment fully engaged and connected is powerful. Efficiency, productivity, enhances when we are focused and can achieve much more in our lives with less mindful clutter.

➢ **Empathy**: Embracing the new era of this next generation you are building. Being sensitive and open to the feelings of others. Understanding the perception and the perspective of the other person. This is the art of finding the reasons behind the decision making, and thought process of others. With kindness and warmth, this is the new era of leadership.

➢ **Compassion**: The understanding to have self-compassion, that you are doing the best that you can. Removing the pressures that we sometimes place on ourselves that can cause overdoing, overachieving, overanalyzing. This removes anxiety, manages stress better, allows for empathy and kindness, and a more heart-centered approach to solve some of the most challenging and complex problems in our lives with even the smallest ounce of compassion.

➤ **Adaptability:** Being flexible is one of the single most valuable characteristics you can embody to move with the seasons of life. The challenges of the moment, the sometimes uncalled for unexplainable situations that arise that test your core strength. The ability for you pivot, change direction, shift your mindset and become fluid with the unexpected is remarkable in not only in leadership of life, but more importantly to stabilize your internal foundation, as well as your influence on others.

➤ **Vulnerability:** One of the single most game-changing characteristics you can encompass, this will change your world. It is traditionally seen as a sign of weakness. In some cultures, and parts of the world, in fact, it is discouraged to lead from a transparent lens. However, when you are able to be vulnerable and showcase a more "human" and relatable side to you, it offers humility, trust, and respect that is instantly gained. It offers a tremendous opportunity for us to realize we are imperfect beings. Celebrate flaws and champion some aspects that make you human which is desperately something that offers more collaboration and more cohesion with families, businesses, communities, and societies as a whole.

➤ **Resilience:** This is the understanding that adversity is a part of life. Embrace the tenacity and fierce capacity to rise up again and again, in the face of the natural ebb and flow of life. In every single life there will be dark times, and it's not about avoiding them altogether, it's about understanding how to navigate through the challenging aspects of life and embrace some of the toughest parts along the road. Everyone will have them to some degree or another. It is not about being the victim, but rather opening oneself to life's valuable lessons that strengthen your core as a human as a result. Utilize the silver lining in each scenario, so that you can make better decisions as a result.

EmotionalGRIT RESOURCES

For more information on bringing EmotionalGRIT to your businesses, companies, and organizations, check out the EmotionalGRIT full suite at www.emotionalgrit.com. As part of the community, you will have access to free resources, online courses, and GlobalGRIT live events.

Dr. Neeta speaks and leads THRIVE workshops, company leadership retreats, and deep dives through the GlobalGRIT Institute, which teaches EmotionalGRIT practices around the world. For more on how you can create a more heart-centered and humanistic revolution in your world and business ethos, contact Neeta@globalgritinstitute.com.

Bibliography

Chapter One
- "Director's Blog: Mortality and Mental Disorders," accessed August 17, 2016, http://www.nimh.nih.gov/about/director/2015/mortality-and-mental-disorders.shtml.
- "Life Event, Stress and Illness", accessed August 17, 2016, http://www.ncbi.nlm.nih.gov/pmc/articles/PMC3341916/.
- "Stress management", accessed August 17, 2016, http://www.mayoclinic.org/healthy-lifestyle/stress-management/expert-answers/stress/faq-20058233.

Chapter Two
- "How To Lead with Empathy (and When Not To)," accessed August 17, 2016, http://www.inc.com/john-baldoni/how-to-lead-with-empathy-and-when-not-to.html.
- "71% Of Millennials Want Their Co-Workers To Be A 'Second Family'," accessed August 17, 2016, http://www.businessinsider.com/millennials-want-to-be-connected-to-their-coworkers-2013-6.
- "Millennials: 'We expect to keep working till the day we die'," accessed August 17, 2016, https://www.weforum.org/agenda/2016/05/millennials-working-till-we-die/.
- "Which companies are best at empathy?", accessed August 17, 2016, https://www.weforum.org/agenda/2015/12/which-companies-are-best-at-empathy/.
- Maslow, 1954, Motivation and Personality, pp.xii-xiii

Chapter Three
- http://ccare.stanford.edu/
- "Social Intelligence and the Biology of Leadership," accessed August 17, 2016, http://www.seedsofcompassion.org/who/

Chapter 4

- "Testing for Joy and Grit? Schools Nationwide Push to Measure Students' Emotional Skills," last modified March 2, 2016, accessed August 17, 2016, http://www.nytimes.com/2016/03/01/us/testing-for-joy-and-grit-schools-nationwide-push-to-measure-students-emotional-skills.html?_r=0

- "Own our history. Change the story," accessed August 17, 2016, http://brenebrown.com/2015/06/18/own-our-history-change-the-story/.

- http://brenebrown.com/research

- Goodstartups.com

- Lerner, Jennifer & Keltner, Dascher. "Beyond valence: Toward a model of emotion-specific influences on judgement and choice". Accessed on August 15th 2016. http://ist-socrates.berkeley.edu/~keltner/publications/lerner.keltner.2000.pdf

- Bettman, R. James, Mary Frances Luce, and John W. Payne (1998), "Constructive Consumer Choice Processes," Journal of Consumer Research, 25 (December), 187-217.

Chapter 5

- "How Music Affects Our Moods," accessed August 17, 2016, http://www.healthline.com/health-news/mental-listening-to-music-lifts-or-reinforces-mood-051713.

- "Trying to be Happier Works When Listening to Upbeat Music, According to MU Research," accessed August 17, 2016, http://munews.missouri.edu/news-releases/2013/0514-trying-to-be-happier-works-when-listening-to-upbeat-music-according-to-mu-research/.

- Yuna Ferguson, & Sheldon, Kenneth. "Trying to be happier really can work: Two experimental studies." Page 23-33 | Received 06 Jun 2012, Accepted 29 Oct 2012, Published online: 19 Dec 2012

- "Frank Lipman: Alternative Medicine Man," accessed August 17, 2016, http://www.mensjournal.com/magazine/frank-lipman-alternative-medicine-man-20120723.
- "What is the function of the various brainwaves?," accessed August 17, 2016, http://www.scientificamerican.com/article/what-is-the-function-of-t-1997-12-22/.
- Indian J Physiol Pharmacol 1998; 42 (4) : 467-472
- http://www.ibfnetwork.com/, International Breathwork Foundation
- "The Art and Science of Breathing," accessed August 17, 2016, http://www.drweil.com/drw/u/ART02039/the-art-and-science-of-breathing.html
- "The Health Benefits of Journaling", accessed August 17, 2016, http://psychcentral.com/lib/the-health-benefits-of-journaling/.
- "Writing to heal," accessed August 17, 2016, http://www.apa.org/monitor/jun02/writing.aspx.
- "Aromatherapy," accessed August 17, 2016, http://www.takingcharge.csh.umn.edu/explore-healing-practices/aromatherapy.

Chapter 6
- "Snakes in the MRI Machine: A Study of Courage," accessed August 17, 2016, http://www.scientificamerican.com/article/snakes-in-the-mri-machine/.
- "The Science of Forgiveness," accessed August 17, 2016, http://www.baylor.edu/ifl/christianreflection/Forgiveness bookreviewMeek.pdf.
- www.goodstartups.com
- "Forgiveness: Letting go of grudges and bitterness," accessed August 17, 2016, http://www.mayoclinic.org/healthy-lifestyle/adult-health/in-depth/forgiveness/art-20047692.

- "Teach girls bravery, not perfection," accessed August 17, 2016, https://www.ted.com/talks/reshma_saujani_teach_girls_bravery_not_perfection/transcript?language=en.
- "Why Women Don't Apply for Jobs Unless They're 100% Qualified," accessed August 17, 2016, https://hbr.org/2014/08/why-women-dont-apply-for-jobs-unless-theyre-100-qualified/.

Chapter 7
- Robbins, Tony: *Unleash the power within*
- "Curiosity Prepares the Brain for Better Learning," accessed August 17, 2016, http://www.scientificamerican.com/article/curiosity-prepares-the-brain-for-better-learning/.
- "Curiosity: It Helps Us Learn, But Why?," accessed August 17, 2016, http://www.npr.org/sections/ed/2014/10/24/357811146/curiosity-it-may-have-killed-the-cat-but-it-helps-us-learn.
- "Serotonin: 9 Questions and Answers," accessed August 17, 2016, http://www.webmd.com/depression/features/serotonin.
- Shonstrom, Erik. *Wild Curiosity*
- "The Delicate Art of Pushing Back," accessed August 17, 2016, http://www.wsj.com/articles/SB10001424127887323482504578227613937854612.

Chapter 8
- "Don't Let Your Ego Hijack Your Leadership Effectiveness," accessed August 17, 2016, http://www.fastcompany.com/1840932/dont-let-your-ego-hijack-your-leadership-effectiveness.
- "Ryan Holiday: How Ego Makes Business Leaders Less Successful," accessed August 17, 2016, http://www.forbes.com/sites/danschawbel/2016/06/14/ryan-holiday-how-ego-makes-business-leaders-less-successful/#317ee9514906.
- http://www.pbs.org/newshour/bb/business-jan-june13-makingsense_06-20/.
- http://www.cbs.mpg.de/mitarbeiter/singer

- "Empathy Is the Secret to Writing That Sells, According to Science," accessed August 17, 2016, http://www.inc.com/kaleigh-moore/empathy-is-the-secret-to-writing-that-sells-according-to-science.html.
- "The Science of Compassion," last modified, August 7, 2012, accessed August 17, 2016, http://www.huffingtonpost.com/james-r-doty-md/science-of-compassion_b_1578284.html

Chapter 9
- "Afraid Of Being 'Found Out?' How To Overcome Impostor Syndrome," accessed August 17, 2016, http://www.forbes.com/sites/margiewarrell/2014/04/03/impostor-syndrome/#65627ef7eb9d.
- Waters, E., Corcoran, D. & Anafarta, M. (2005) 'Attachment, Other Relationships, and the Theory that All Good Things Go Together' Human Development 48:80–84 "," accessed August 17, 2016,
- J. Basic. Appl. Sci. Res., 2(2)1793-1802, 2012 Shohreh Ghorbanshirodi
- Meisel, Ari. *Less Doing*
- "Compassionate Leaders – a new breed?…," accessed August 17, 2016, http://www.thechangeforum.com/The_Compassionate_Leader.htm.

Chapter 10
- "Why Flexibility is a Key Leadership Asset," accessed August 17, 2016, http://www.forefrontmag.com/2014/07/why-flexibility-is-a-key-leadership-asset/.
- http://corporateathleteedge.com/aug13/ISSUE NO.14.
- http://iveybusinessjournal.com/publication/the-resilient-leader-why-eq-matters/.
- "THE RESILIENT LEADER: WHY EQ MATTERS," accessed August 17, 2016, https://www.psychologytoday.com/blog/communication-success/201407/the-problem-perfectionism-how-truly-succeed

Chapter 11
- "Can't Get Therapy? Try Gratitude and Kindness," accessed August 17, 2016, http://greatergood.berkeley.edu/article/item/cant_get_the rapy_try_gratitude_and_kindness.
- Local and Non-Local Effects of Coherent Heart Frequencies on Conformational Changes of DNA, Glen Rein, PhD , Rollin McCraty, PhD 01/01/2001

Chapter 12 -Chapter 14
- https://www.ashoka.org/video/interview-bill-drayton-ceo-and-founder-ashoka.
- "TINA ROTH EISENBERG Founder/CEO at Creative Mornings and Tattly. Living in Brooklyn.," accessed August 17, 2016, https://creativemornings.com/people/swissmiss.
- "Rainn Wilson on SoulPancake and Social Media," accessed August 17, 2016, https://www.entrepreneur.com/article/223277.
- www.gamechangers500.com
- "Gabriel Baldinucci," accessed August 17, 2016, http://singularityu.org/bio/gabriel-baldinucci/.
- "Creating Shared Value," accessed August 17, 2016, https://hbr.org/2011/01/the-big-idea-creating-shared-value.

About the Author

"Dr. Neeta Bhushan is transforming the next frontier of leadership. She is multi-dimensional, using connection and abounding promise to shift the dialogue of human potential. She inspires millions to understand their emotions during an ever changing and increasingly chaotic world.—Vinay Rai, Author, Philanthropist, Billionaire, Founder Rai University, India.

Neeta is an emotional intelligence advocate, host of the *Revolutionary Leadership* podcast, and is founder of the Global GRIT Institute. Neeta's personal journey through navigating death, cancer, domestic violence, and divorce and how she overcomes extraordinary adversity began her quest to embark on her own self-discovery. Leaving her traditional career as a cosmetic dentist to embark on global advocacy championing emotional awareness and new thought leadership.

After spreading transformational wisdom and inspiration to top level CEOs, business executives around the world, notable changemakers from various sectors and truly understanding human dynamics in traveling to over 45 countries, Neeta's greater mission is to create a more heart-centered humanistic society realizing the capacity for change lies within the mastery of our emotional GRIT. Using empathy based solutions to push forth global impact in our communities and thereby shifting economies as a result.

www.neetabhushan.com . @neetabhushan.
www.globalgritinstitute.com

Printed in Poland
by Amazon Fulfillment
Poland Sp. z o.o., Wrocław

49010749R00179